Ottawa
A CAPITAL CITY

Published by: Heritage Media Corp., PO Box 131270, Carlsbad, California 92013
ISBN: 1-58967-004-03
Library of Congress Control Number: 2001007093
First Edition,

Table of Contents

Bytown and its environs astonishes me; I have walked ten miles to view the river scenery and, though much fatigued, am highly gratified. This place has a large trade and will increase with the prosperity of the country round it; nature seems to have destined it for the site of a great city.

—*William Lyon Mackenzie,* October 11, 1851

Introductory Essay

BY JIM WATSON

William Lyon Mackenzie–a leading ublic figure in Canadian history couldn't have said it any better.

I, like many other residents of Ottawa, was not born and raised here, but chose this city as my new hometown. Having lived in small towns and big cities, I qucikly realized that Ottawa has the best of both worlds. A former prime minister of Canada once called this country a community of communities. I believe Ottawa can best be described as a community of neighbourhoods.

When I first arrived in Ottawa to attend Carleton University, what struck me was the sheer beauty of our nation's capital. Words cannot describe seeing the sun set behind the Peace Tower and the Gothic Parliament buildings, or the sheer exhilaration of skating the full length of the Rideau Canal in February.

Ottawa has small-town charm and values, yet all of the amenities of a major urban city befitting the capital of a G-8 nation.

Ottawa is also a wonderfully multicultural community that is a microcosm of the world around us. Walking down Somerset Street has the feel of a commercial area of Beijing, while touring Preston Street brings you back in time to a village in Italy.

Ottawa: Capital City Compromise

Canadians are well known around the world as great peacekeepers–people who will seek out consensus and compromise before conflict. It is not surprising, therefore, that the choice of Ottawa as our capital was just that–a compromise.

In 1840, when Upper and Lower Canada were joined in union, the capital shifted between Toronto and Québec City every four years. Bitter divisions resulted when, in 1856, Québec City was voted the new capital. To avoid an impasse, Queen Victoria was asked to make the definitive decision. The governor general at the time, Sir Edmund Heath, said that Ottawa "will be accepted by the majority of Upper and Lower Canada as a fair compromise." Queen Victoria concurred, and in January 1858 she wrote, "Ottawa must indeed be a beautiful situation and all the detached descriptions must tend to confirm the impressions that the choice is the right one."

Located at the confluence of the Ottawa and Rideau rivers, the city of Ottawa stands both as a reminder of Canada's origins and as a beacon for its future development. As the capital city, Ottawa is in an ideal position to lead by example–to show that past, present, and future can come together to form something special. This symbolism is evident even in a physical sense, as the city spans the Ottawa River–which is shared by the provinces of Québec and Ontario–and makes Ottawa emblematic of the two national cultures that founded Canada.

Up until 2001, the population of Ottawa proper was just under 350,000. Just prior to 2001, the Provincial Government imposed a municipal amalgamation that saw 11 local municipalities and the regional government merge to create the new City of Ottawa, with a population close to 800,000–making it the fourth-largest city in Canada.

Across the river, the Québec government followed suit and passed legislation to create one new city from several smaller municipalities. The newly created city of Gatineau has a population of approximately 225,000.

Business and Quality of Life

One of Ottawa's great strengths is its quality of life–a low crime rate; lots of green space, lakes, and rivers; good schools and hospitals; and less urban stress and sprawl than most other North American cities. The Corporate Resources Group, a relocation and site selection management company based in Switzerland, has named Ottawa as number six on its list of world cities with an outstanding quality of life.

Indeed, the quality of life here has attracted a number of prominent corporate citizens. The major local industries are advanced technology, tourism, retail, and services.

High-tech firms–representing the most recent of these major industrial sectors–have found Ottawa to be a congenial and convenient home. Among this group are major global corporations such as Alcatel, Corel Corporation, Nortel Networks, Mitel Corporation, JDS Uniphase, and Cognos Inc. These are but the largest and best known among the city's more than 1,000 high-tech corporate citizens. In all, these companies employ an estimated 75,000

workers, and produce goods that are sold worldwide. In fact, some 90 percent of the products that these corporations are responsible for are exported beyond Canada's borders.

High tech is now the second-largest employer in Ottawa–after the federal government–and if it were not for the economic downturn of 2001, high tech would probably have become number one.

Why the city attracts so many home-grown and international high-tech firms is both obvious and historical. Obvious, because the quality of life that Ottawa offers young professionals makes it easy to attract people to a community like Ottawa. Historical, because the government of Canada was the first pioneer that invested in research and development in this country.

Through the efforts of the National Research Council (NRC), companies like Bell Northern Research were formed. Technology companies wanted to be near R and D incubators like the NRC, and they also needed to be near the government regulators and purchasers like the Department of National Defence and Industry Canada. Other vibrant and growing sectors in Ottawa are the life sciences and biotechnology. Again, proximity to the federal regulators, such as Health Canada, makes Ottawa an ideal location for these types of leading-edge companies.

Another primary business sector is tourism. Each year, some 4 million tourists visit Ottawa, drawn to the capital city to enjoy Parliament Hill, the parks, the historic buildings, and the numerous attractions that form a strong arts community and a thriving cultural centre. Close to 20,000 residents are employed in the tourism industry, and Ottawa is ideally situated between Canada's two biggest tourism cities, Montréal and Toronto.

Ottawa is quite literally surrounded by alluring parks and wildlife in the form of an "emerald necklace"–a green belt that features a continuous network of interconnected public parks, forests, and wetlands that circle the city. Here, in this unique green space, is an enticing array of bicycle and jogging paths, cross-country ski trails, and

walking paths. Another unique area that attracts visitors from all over is the 500-hectre Central Experimental Farm, the only urban farm of its kind in North America.

Across the Ottawa River from the city, one is surrounded by the spectacular Gatineau hills–home to great hiking in the summer, great skiing in the winter, and an explosion of colour in the fall.

Some of the country's most important museums and cultural facilities are located in Ottawa. The Parliament buildings themselves are a national treasure, and are a year-round attraction for Canadians. Located on Parliament Hill, with a fine view of the Ottawa River, the Parliament buildings are comprised of the Peace Tower–which is the dominant and most memorable feature of Parliament–along with the east, centre, and west blocks. The centre block was destroyed by fire in 1916, but was rebuilt and reopened in 1920 in a larger and grander incarnation. In addition to the Parliament buildings, Wellington Street is home to the National War Memorial and the Tomb of the Unknown Soldier; the Supreme Court Building; and the National Library and Archives. Another important thoroughfare is Sussex Drive, which is lined with public buildings, including the prime minister's residence and the new U.S. Embassy.

Rideau Hall, the residence of the governor general, is another oft-visited historic structure, as are the Anglican and Roman Catholic cathedrals, Bytown Museum, Canadian Museum of Nature, National Gallery of Canada, National Arts Centre, Canada Science and Technology Museum, Dominion Observatory, Bank of Canada Building, Royal Canadian Mint, Canadian Museum of Contemporary Photography, and the most popular tourist gathering spot–Byward Market, named after the genius who built the Rideau Canal, Colonel John By.

Other tourist attractions that shouldn't be missed include the changing of the guard ceremony from late June through late August on Parliament Hill. This impressive ceremony–a replica of the ceremony at Buckingham Palace–attracts thousands of visitors every day.

The world-famous RCMP Musical Ride has its stables and training grounds in Ottawa, where visitors can tour the site and on certain days watch the Musical Ride's sunset ceremony, complete with bagpipes and officers in red serge.

Near the mouth of this river another coming from the south, and at its mouth there is a wonderful waterfall; for, from a height of 20 or 25 fathoms, it falls with such impetuosity that it forms an archway nearly 400 yards in width. The Indians, for the fun of it, pass underneath this without getting wet, except for the spray made by the falling water. There is an island in the middle of this river, which, like all the land round about, is covered with pines and white cedar.

–Samuel de Champlain (French explorer)

One of the earliest recollections of explorers travelling to this part of Canada was in 1610. The meeting of the Ottawa and Rideau rivers was an area first inhabited by the Algonquin and Outaouais–Indian tribes that hunted and lived off the land.

Early explorers who set foot in this part of the world included Samuel de Champlain, Pierre Esprit Radisson, Médard Chouart des Groseilliers, Sir Martin Frobisher, Sir Alexander Mackenzie, and Thomas Douglas, earl of Selkirk.

As the region became better known, it quickly became an ideal lumber area, with its abundant forests and swiftly moving waters. Probably the area's most significant lumber baron was the American Philemon Wright, who moved to what is now Hull, Québec, in 1800. Wright began the lumber drive down the Ottawa River to Montréal in 1806.

Other famous pioneers of the day include people with surnames like Booth, Sparks, Billings, Perley, Eddy, Rochester, Fisher, and Mackay–all now immortalized through various street names in Ottawa.

When Queen Victoria decided to name Ottawa as capital of the United Province of Canada in 1857, the modest logging community formerly known as Bytown became the governmental centre of one of the Queen's proudest colonies. Ten years later, when the Dominion of Canada was formed, Ottawa was named as its capital. Since then, the city has grown to become one of the world's most charming and accessible capital cities, one in

which the city and the government have evolved in tandem to create a special and unique environment. Now, nearly 150 years later, we are happy to announce that the Queen was right in her choice.

The city of Ottawa itself was founded in 1826 by Lieutenant-Colonel John By (hence the rather immodest name of Bytown), an engineer who found himself in the area as builder of the Rideau Canal, originally a military fortification, which today splits and defines the city.

The entire Rideau Canal is 125 miles long and connects Ottawa with the city of Kingston, Ontario. Construction began in 1827 and was completed–for the most part–six years later. The canal includes 47 locks and 24 dams, and was built as a way to protect the free flow of soldiers within Canada from American attack.

In 1854, with the canal mainly completed and John By no longer the centre of attention, the city was renamed Ottawa, after the Algonquian-speaking group of Native Americans. This proved to be an auspicious move, because it took only three years for Queen Victoria to realize that this was, indeed, the ideal place to locate the capital.

Although a successful lumber settlement since 1800–and a successful trading post for decades before that–Ottawa's selection as Canada's capital city sealed its fate as a government, rather than a woodland, centre. However, the lumber industry continued to flourish until the early years of the 20th century, and declined simultaneously with Canada's emergence as a world power.

In the 20th century, Ottawa's energy was directed toward governance rather than lumber mills or factories. This continued until the 1990s, when the city was once again discovered as an ideal locale for industry, this time of the high-tech variety. Here, the digital electronics and advanced technology companies found a welcoming local government, ready access to the federal government, a highly educated workforce, a progressive spirit, and an outstanding quality of life–just the formula, it seems, to attract advanced engineering, research, and production to the city.

Education

The Ottawa region is home to a number of excellent colleges and universities. Foremost and largest among them are Carleton University and the University of Ottawa.

The University of Ottawa, founded in 1848, remains the city's largest educational institution. Originally known as the College of Bytown, the University of Ottawa comprises some 25,000 students, teaching staff, and support staff in a bilingual environment, making it the largest two-language educational institution in North America. The university prides itself in offering a well-balanced curriculum geared to a wide array of needs and interests, and maintains a role as a major force in the cultural life of the community. The university boasts one of the best medical schools and one of the best law schools in Canada.

Established in 1942, Carleton has gradually evolved and transformed to complement the high-technology industries that have made the NRC their home. The school also has an outstanding reputation for public affairs and management–skills much in demand here in Canada's capital–as well as architecture and journalism.

One of the country's best community colleges, Algonquin College is also located in the nation's capital, as is a relatively new addition, La Cité Collégiale–a French-language college.

Arts, Culture, and Festivals

One might think, from the chilly winter temperatures, that Ottawa is an indoor kind of town. And while a number of the city's most important cultural and recreational events do take place under a roof, others are geared toward drawing residents outdoors–in all seasons–to enjoy the magnificent natural beauty of the region. During the coldest weather, in February, Winterlude provides plenty of opportunities to bundle up and get moving, and remains the largest winter festival in North America, drawing some 600,000 visitors annually. The Rideau Canal features

some of the most scenic ice skating anywhere as it becomes, during the festival, the world's longest ice rink, with small kiosks along the sides selling everything from traditional products like hot chocolate to Ottawa's own BeaverTails–a deliciously flavoured pastry shaped like a beaver tail!

Springtime offers a chance to get out and smell the tulips at the renowned Canadian Tulip Festival, a celebration of the relationship between Canada and the Netherlands. During World War II, following the German invasion of the Netherlands in 1940, Crown Princess Juliana was offered refuge in Canada for herself and her daughters, Beatrix and Irene. On January 19, 1943, Princess Margriet was born at Ottawa's Civic Hospital, and the federal government declared that hospital room as Dutch territory for the day. It was also the only time a foreign flag flew on the Peace Tower.

In appreciation for all that hospitality from Ottawa and Canada, Princess Juliana sent 100,000 tulip bulbs to the city. The flow of tulips from the Netherlands to Ottawa continues to this day.

The Canadian Tulip Festival was the brainchild of noted Ottawa photographer Malak Karsh, who together with the Board of Trade started this tradition, which celebrated its 50th anniversary in 2002. In all, more than 3 million bulbs come to life as the colourful flowers provide nature's signal that summer is upon us.

Another local favorite is Canada Day–July 1–which celebrates the founding of the Dominion of Canada in 1867. An enormous Canada Day celebration is held each year on and around Parliament Hill, with a stunning fireworks display capping the daylong party.

Other popular gatherings include Italian Week; Fête-Caribe; Pride Week; Odawa Pow Wow; Lebanorama; Busker; Central Canada Exhibition; Ottawa International Chamber Music Festival; and blues, jazz, Greek, folk, and hot-air balloon festivals.

For indoor cultural outings, Ottawa offers some 29 museums and dozens of galleries, shops, and libraries. The National Gallery of Canada is located here, housing the world's largest collection of Canadian art. The Canadian Museum of Civilization in Hull offers historical exhibits, while the Canada Science and Technology Museum's

astronomical focus culminates in a look through one of the best public refracting telescopes in North America, offering an ideal view of the heavens. Other notable museums include the Canadian Museum of Nature, Canada Aviation Museum, and Canadian War Museum.

For stage presence, the National Arts Centre has four stages that offer full seasons of outstanding cultural events, including Ottawa's symphony orchestra; Opera Lyra Ottawa, the city's local opera company; and ballet and theatrical productions. The National Arts Centre Orchestra, under the direction of Pinchas Zukerman, is world renowned, and often travels nationally and internationally to rave reviews of their performances.

The local arts and heritage community is alive and vibrant with facilities such as the Arts Court; Great Canadian Theatre Company; Ottawa Little Theatre; La Nouvelle Scène, for French theatre; and surrounding facilities now located in the new City of Ottawa, including Nepean's Centrepoint Theatre and the Ron Maslin Theatre in Kanata.

From a heritage perspective, we boast the Bytown Museum at the foot of the Rideau locks near the historic Chateau Laurier Hotel, and the Billings Estate–home, in 1813, to one of Ottawa's prominent families in the Alta Vista neighbourhood. In fact, local heritage groups are recognized as being some of the most devoted and knowledgeable in their quest to protect our architectural heritage.

Above and beyond being home to all of our political leaders and welcoming world leaders on a regular basis, Ottawa has been home to dozens of internationally known personalities. Among the famous former and current residents of Ottawa are singers Paul Anka, Alanis Morrisette, and Bryan Adams; actors Lorne Green, Tom Green (no relation!), Matthew Perry, and Brendan Fraser; news anchors Peter Jennings (ABC) and Keith Morrison (NBC); photographers–and brothers–Yousuf and Malak Karsh; athletes Barbara Ann Scott, Carolyn Waldo, Glenroy Gilbert, and Elizabeth Manley; and TV personalities Alex Trebek and Rich Little, to name just a few.

Sports and Recreation

Whether sporting events constitute culture or not depends on how good the seats are and how exciting the teams can be. Ottawa is home to the NHL Senators and the 18,500-seat Corel Centre; the Ontario Hockey League's Ottawa 67's; and the AAA Ottawa Lynx of baseball's International League–all of which claim avid fan bases. After a brief hiatus, the Canadian Football League is back playing at Lansdowne Park in the heart of the city.

But the real sports heroes in town are the ones who are outside in all weather, enjoying the games of the season. Junior hockey leagues, skiing, snow shoeing, and curling are popular in the winter, while summertime gives way to cycling (there are some 200 kilometres of paved paths for this purpose in the city alone), canoeing, fishing, swimming, hiking, or just taking a stroll. Whatever the season, whatever the excuse, Ottawans are never at a loss to find a way to get outside, get moving, and enjoy their unique hometown.

A Community of Neighbourhoods

I began this introduction with what I said was the strength of our city–its neighbourhoods. When I was mayor, I most enjoyed the opportunity to go visit residents in their neighbourhoods–to talk and listen to them tell about their dreams and aspirations.

Each part of this new City of Ottawa is filled with distinct and caring communities. The rural villages of Ashton, Munster, Greely, Manotick, Navan, Cumberland, Kars, Vars, Osgoode, Metcalfe, Carp, and Richmond are a joy to visit for a hearty meal or shopping or a country fair. Inner-city neighbourhoods like the Glebe, Old Ottawa South, Centre Town, Westboro, Hintonburg, Preston Street, Lower Town, Sandy Hill, Dow's Lake, Mechanicsville, Golden Triangle, New Edinburgh, Lindenlea, Manor Park, and Rockcliffe Park have a charm that is hard to describe.

Areas like the predominantly French-speaking communities of Vanier and Orleans help to reinforce the two founding nations of this country. And suburban neighbourhoods like Bells Corners, Barrhaven, Kanata, Canterbury, Alta Vista, Gloucester, Overbrook-Forbes, Mooney's Bay, Britannia, Pinecrest, and many others add to the distinctive fabric that is Ottawa.

Ottawa has traditionally been included on lists of the most generous cities in terms of charitable donations and volunteer time for years. It reminds me of the poet Henrik Ibsen's words: "A community is like a ship; everyone ought to be prepared to take the helm."

The people of Ottawa have been taking the helm for close to 150 years–from a small fur-trading and lumber village to a world-class capital. This is why I'm proud to be a resident of this beautiful place I call home.

By Jim Watson

Photo Essay

Photos © William P. McElligott

Gracefully framing the banks of the Ottawa River with such landmarks as Parliament Hill (above, in foreground) and the National Gallery of Canada (opposite, in foreground), Ottawa has expanded significantly since Queen Victoria declared it Canada's capital in 1857. The city is part of the 4,660-square-kilometre National Capital Region–NCR–which comprises the greater City of Ottawa on the Ontario side (above) and the Communauté urbaine de l'Outaouais on the Québec side of the water (opposite).

42
KODAK TX 6043

When the new City of Ottawa first presented its face to the world in January 2001, it was personified by the visage of Mayor Bob Chiarelli (above), elected in November 2000. Although the structure of the city has changed, the government's downtown edifices have not. The Langevin Building (opposite), completed in the late 19th century, still houses offices including that of the Prime Minister.

Parliament Hill, situated on a bluff overlooking the Ottawa River, basks in the light of the Centennial Flame (bottom). Initially lit on January 1, 1967, to commemorate the first century of the country's Confederation, the flame burns as a symbol of Canadian unity. The Peace Tower, (opposite and left) dedicated to Canadians killed in war is the most striking feature of Parliament Hill's Centre Block, which is home to the House of Commons and the Senate.

OWNER OF ALL THEY SURVEY: A statue of Samuel de Champlain stands on the south shore of the Ottawa River, which the French explorer navigated as early as 1613. The figure holds aloft a replica of an astrolabe—an instrument used to measure the altitude of sun and stars—that Champlain lost during one of his journeys. At the eastern entrance to the Sparks Street Mall, Bruce Garner's sculpture *Territorial Prerogative* reminds visitors to the crowded shopping area that nature is still a force to be reckoned with.

THE CHANGING OF THE GUARD is more than just a figure of speech on Parliament Hill: during the summer months, the Ceremonial Guard of the Canadian Forces presents the military pageant on a daily basis (OPPOSITE AND BOTTOM). In June 2001, the changing of the guard was also performed as part of the ceremony for the Chief of Defence Staff change of command. Adrienne Clarkson, Governor General and Commander-in-Chief of the Canadian Forces, presided over the ceremony, held on Festival Plaza in front of City Hall (TOP).

Both in times of peace and times of conflict, memorials scattered throughout Ottawa remind residents and visitors of the sacrifices made by fellow citizens. Canada regularly provides support for the United Nations' peacekeeping missions, a fact reflected by "Reconciliation," which stands outside the National Gallery of Canada and honours military and civilian peacekeepers (top). The Canadian War Museum, next door to the National Gallery, stands guard over an astounding array of military paraphernalia, from uniforms and medals to tanks and other vehicles (bottom). Less than a kilometre away, the National War Memorial in Confederation Square pays a lasting tribute to those Canadians lost in war (opposite).

July 1 is flagged on calendars across the nation, in celebration of the creation of Canada's federal government in 1867. Local Canada Day festivities kick into colourfully high gear with fireworks, food, and music, and leave their mark on the faces of Ottawa and its residents.

495
496

As a rule, Ottawans leap at the chance to show their pride in the region's incredible ethnic diversity. The annual Cultures Galore Festival, held in Confederation Park on Canada Day, offers a bright and energetic display of traditional dances, music, and food from around the world. And just 80 kilometres from Ottawa, the Glengarry Highland Games in Maxville (right and opposite, top right) draw more than 25,000 people each year to watch or participate in the event's contests and performances.

Numerous political dignitaries have made public appearances in the country's capital, but who's counting? Among them are (FROM OPPOSITE LEFT) former South African President Nelson Mandela; Vincente Fox, President of Mexico–who met with Governor General Adrienne Clarkson during a 2001 visit to Canada; and Palestinian leader Yasar Arafat.

OTTAWA'S MULTICULTURAL POPulation is accompanied by a panoply of religious faiths, from Buddhists to Sikhs to Muslims, Jews, and Christians. This rich mixture of heritages provides added depth to the Ottawan tapestry, particularly when groups pool their prayers for tolerance and peace (OPPOSITE BOTTOM).

FROM HIGH SCHOOL FUNCTIONS to theatrical performances, there's never a dull moment in Ottawa, where cultural offerings have reached jaw-dropping proportions. Interspersed with performances of tried-and-true favourites like *The Mikado*, such innovations as the Odyssey Theatre's adaptation of Edgar Allan Poe's poem "The Raven" (OPPOSITE BOTTOM) round out a dramatic spectrum of entertainment.

Deep devotion is a tenet of the Catholic faith—and just what was required for the 1999 restoration of Ottawa's historic Notre Dame Cathedral. Upon completion of the work, Archbishop Marcel Gervais (above) showed his thanks by holding a private mass for all involved in the project. More than 200 people worked with religious fervor to restore the church, performing tasks from repairing roofs to creating new gold-leaf stars for the vaulted ceiling. Originally completed in 1847, the church is the oldest in the National Capital Region.

THE MUSICAL EVENTS IN OTTAWA can take your breath away. Since 1969, the National Arts Centre, or NAC, has hosted dance and musical performances on one of the largest stages in North America. Events range from evenings with the National Arts Centre Orchestra–which has performed with guests such as Jessye Norman (TOP, ON LEFT)–to regular visits from professional ballet companies, including Les Grands Ballets Canadiens de Montreal (OPPOSITE BOTTOM). The internationally recognized concert pianist Dang Thai Son, a resident of Montreal, has also made a number of appearances in the city (BOTTOM).

MOSH PIT, MUD PIT, OR GRASSY knoll: it's not the location of the seating that matters so much as who's on the stage. At the Cisco Systems Bluesfest, concert-goers can choose from multiple stages showcasing blues and gospel musicians from around the globe. The multiday festival's past rosters have included Blues Traveler's John Popper (TOP LEFT), classic bluesman John Hammond (TOP RIGHT), and the legendary James Brown (OPPOSITE, BOTTOM RIGHT).

IN OTTAWA, AS IN OTHER CITIES of note, many find that the magic is in the music. The area's night life boasts a number of clubs that attract musicians from every genre, including Charlie Gordon, whose smoky jazz trumpet has earned him a steady fan base (TOP), and native Ottawan Alec Walkington, a jazz bassist now based in Montreal (OPPOSITE).

A SHOWER OF COINS MAY NOT BE a sure thing at a casino, but having fun is a bet anyone can win, whether glittering like a star or choosing to remain anonymous. The Rideau Carleton Raceway in Gloucester, some 20 minutes south of Ottawa, features live harness racing from February through October, as well as the Slot Casino, open year-round. Just four kilometres north of Parliament Hill, the Casino de Hull provides patrons with more than 60 gaming tables and 1,800 slot machines.

FASHION THAT LOOKS GOOD ON paper: Proving that Ottawa is a model city in more ways than one, designer Richard Robinson, who founded the Richard Robinson Academy of Fashion Design several decades ago, holds an annual gala to showcase his students' work (LEFT AND OPPOSITE TOP). Marlen Cowpland (OPPOSITE BOTTOM, CENTRE), who hosts television's "Celebrity Pets," knows–along with husband Michael, son Roman, and canine companion Bunny–that her sense of style helps keep her in the pink.

PUT ON SOME COMFORTABLE shoes, pack a basket of provisions, and take a tour of all that Ottawa's many museums–with their equally diverse holdings and architecture–have to offer. At the National Gallery of Canada (TOP), designed by Moshe Safdie, the emphasis is on Canadian works, and permanent collections include more than 1,300 pieces of Inuit art. Inside the Victoria Memorial Museum Building of the Canadian Museum of Nature (BOTTOM), the ordinary sights of downtown fall away as visitors travel through 4 billion years of the earth's history, illustrated by dinosaur, rock and mineral, and other exhibitions. Douglas Cardinal's geologically influenced design for the Canadian Museum of Civilization in Hull (OPPOSITE) welcomes the curious to an in-depth history of Canada's cultural groups, illustrated by nearly 4 million artifacts.

Crafts, ceremonial dress, and traditional music and dancing are all part of the public face of members of the area's First Nations. During Canada Day performances by First Nations Dance (right), Ottawans of all backgrounds gain some insight into the lives and heritage of Canada's aboriginal peoples.

IT TAKES MORE THAN WALLS AND a roof to make a home, but even those basic ingredients lend themselves to all manner of variations. In addition to its many restaurants and shops, downtown's ByWard Market includes a number of courtyards, one of which features the façade of an old tin house, now hung on the wall of another structure (ABOVE RIGHT). Stately homes and gardens a few blocks away on King Edward Avenue (ABOVE LEFT) offer an excuse for a pleasant stroll, and–a few minutes south of downtown–the Billings Estate Museum's buildings, cemetery, and 1820s furnishings offer insight into the lives of some of Ottawa's first permanent settlers (OPPOSITE).

FROM THE CLASSIC TO THE ULTRA-modern, downtown Ottawa's hotels offer the ultimate in hospitality and luxury. The landmark Fairmont Château Laurier (LEFT), at the very edge of the Rideau Canal, comprises 425 rooms, each with a spectacular view of the city. At ARC The.Hotel (OPPOSITE), scores of amenities–including a library–underscore the facility's attention to detail.

OTTAWA'S PUBLIC SCULPTURE walks a fine line between traditional and abstract works–and everything in-between, best characterized by the whimsical work "Balancing," outside the National Arts Centre (ABOVE). From Parliament Hill, where a likeness of Queen Elizabeth gazes down at lawmakers and curious passers-by alike (OPPOSITE, TOP RIGHT), to the Garden of the Provinces and more modern pieces such as "Twelve Points in a Classical Balance" (OPPOSITE, BOTTOM RIGHT), Ottawa's outdoors is a showcase for art.

STATENS JÄRNVÄGAR.
909
E2
1907

So long as the Hull-Chelsea-Wakefield Steam Train is still winding its way along the Gatineau River, the Ottawa region is unlikely ever to run out of steam (top and opposite). The five-hour scenic tour includes a two-hour stopover in the village of Wakefield, Québec, some 30 kilometres north of Ottawa. Those who prefer to explore a steam train without leaving the city can climb aboard at the Canada Science and Technology Museum (bottom), just 10 minutes from downtown.

Some trees in Ontario and Québec provide more than shade and lovely autumnal foliage: they're also a vital part of the region's economy. Milled for lumber (bottom) or pulped for paper (top), wood is a primary export for these provinces. On a sweeter note, Jim Stewart of Stewart's Maple Products in Almonte taps into trees' inner resources each year when the sap is running (opposite).

FROM FRESH FRUIT AND FLOWERS to casual and upscale eateries, there's always something exciting on the menu at ByWard Market. A short distance from Parliament Hill, and other downtown attractions, the market also offers a number of eclectic shops and a bustling night life.

When it comes to outdoor beauty, autumn is a golden time. Whether capturing the best of the season on canvas or simply enjoying the sunshine and brisk air, Ottawans know how to enjoy the fruits of the season.

There's no need to tiptoe through these tulips. Every May, the Canadian Tulip Festival bursts into bloom, attracting people from around the world to view the millions of flowers. The largest festival of its kind in the world, the event has been a perennial favourite since 1953. Celebrated photographer Malak (opposite right), who has participated in the festival since the beginning, has watched it grow through the years to include concerts, floats, and the occasional tulip-shaped hot-air balloon (above left).

EVERY YEAR, THE GATINEAU HOT Air Balloon Festival draws some 200,000 spectators to the region. Pilots–whether racing or hovering–get a bird's-eye view of the more down-to-earth segment of the event, which features musicians, magicians, acrobats, and other performers.

Contemporary
Photography

With easy access to such major waterways as the Ottawa and Rideau rivers, as well as the Rideau Canal and Dow's Lake, residents of and visitors to Ottawa can make waves nearly any way they choose. Sailing, rafting, and kayaking boast devotees of all ages and skill levels, and preferences range from calm to white water.

OTTAWANS DON'T GET BENT OUT of shape when it comes to rigorous exercise: in fact, some residents even make a living at it. Locally based fitness consultant Ginette Deslauriers (TOP, IN FOREGROUND), fuelled by the success of her television show *Kardio Knockout,* has designed the Urban Tai Chi program. The regimen and its accompanying video give new life to the idea of survival of the fittest.

Weaving through motorized traffic or racing against each other, cyclists view their two-wheeled vehicles as sources of freedom, of income–and, occasionally, of pain. Annual races in the Ottawa region include the Tim Hortons National Mountain Bike Championships (left) and the bicycle race that forms one of the highlights of Italian Week (right). In a different league altogether, courier John Nagle (opposite) of Speedy Messenger Service keeps to the streets for his daily rides.

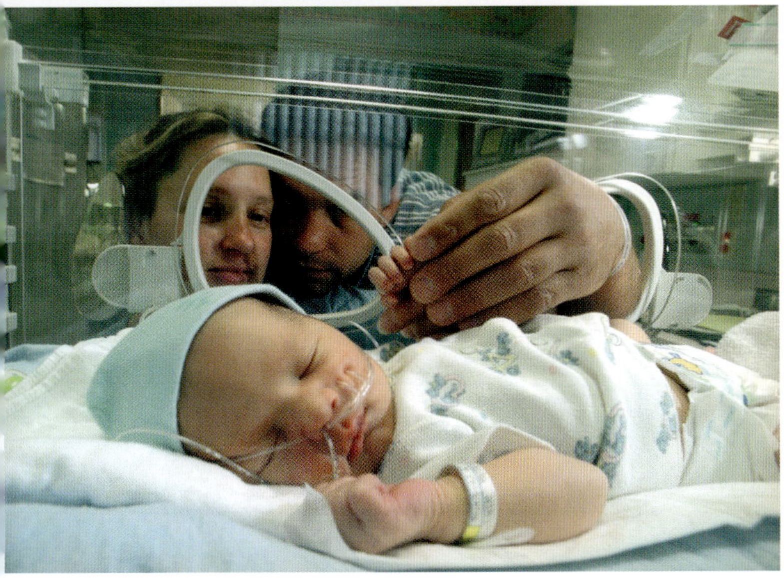

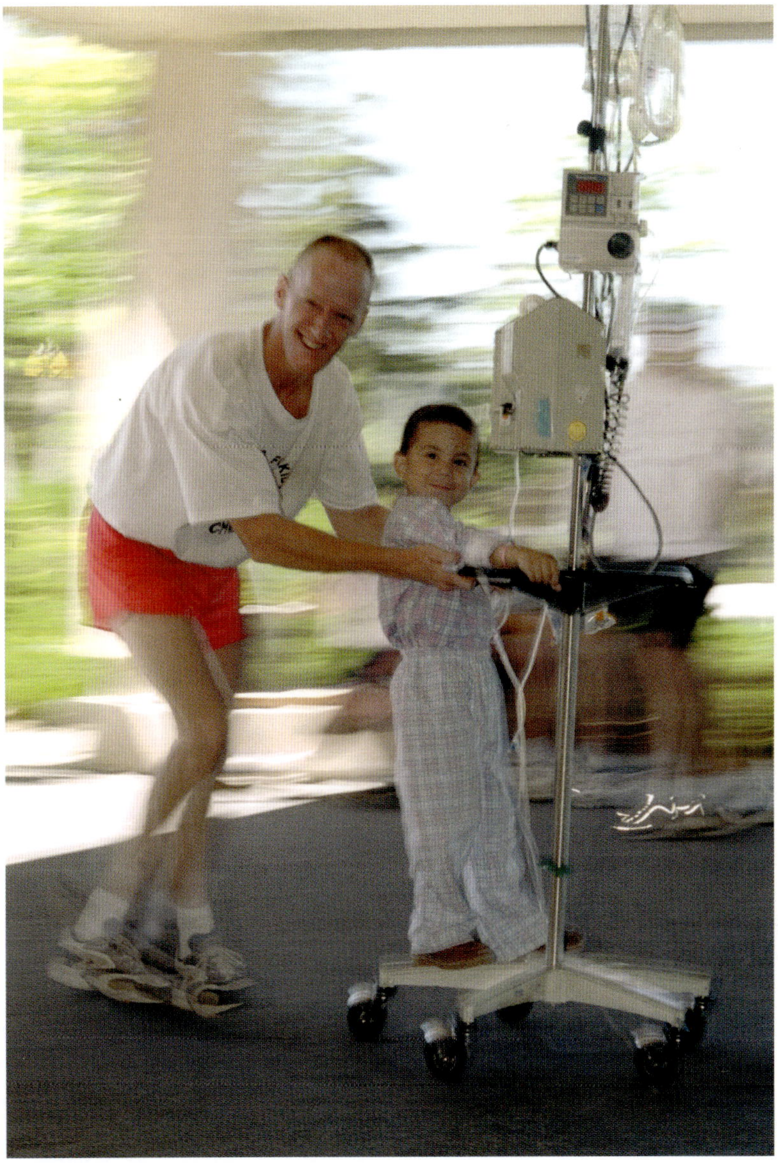

HEALTH CARE FACILITIES AFFILIATED with the University of Ottawa work to promote the health of citizens of all ages. At the University of Ottawa Heart Institute (TOP LEFT), the emphases are education about, prevention of, and research into heart disease. The Ottawa Hospital's three campuses feature such highly personalized units as the Rich Little Special Care Nursery (BOTTOM LEFT) and the Ottawa First Episode Psychosis Program, which is under the leadership of Medical Director Paul Roy (OPPOSITE). The Children's Hospital of Eastern Ontario, or CHEO, treats some 6,000 young inpatients each year and is the recipient of funds raised in the annual CHEO Run For Kids involving participants such as Corporal Willard Smith (RIGHT, ON LEFT).

BAUER
BAUER

THE OTTAWA SENATORS CLUB isn't the only hockey game in town. The Ottawa 67's, the Ontario Hockey League team (TOP AND OPPOSITE, BOTTOM LEFT), draw loyal fans to the Ottawa Civic Centre for their junior hockey league games. Off the ice, the Senators maintain community ties through events such as the annual Dodge/NHL SuperSkills competition, where team members–and aspiring young stars–work to raise funds for Ronald McDonald House as part of the Hockey Fights Cancer and NHLPA's Goals and Dreams Fund (OPPOSITE, BOTTOM RIGHT). In 2000, hockey great Wayne Gretzky came to town–not to catch a game, but to suit up those interested in his new line of clothing (OPPOSITE, TOP).

CITY TAKEN BY STORM
Oh bother! Pooh's one troubled bear

NEWS OTHER THAN THE WEATHER may sometimes get buried during winter, but life goes on around Ottawa. Ice causes aggravation for some, but for others, it forms the basis for a work of art—particularly during the Winterlude festival in February (RIGHT).

◆ © WILLIAM P. MCELLIGOTT

The Rideau Canal is busy during every season, but it is seldom more beautiful than during the winter, when it freezes and becomes the world's longest ice-skating rink. Some eight kilometres of the canal are open to the public, providing plenty of elbow room for casual skating, impromptu races, and moments of a more personal nature (pages 100-101).

On the Rideau Canal

Canada Post

THE LAST TWO DECADES OF CANADA POST'S HISTORY ARE AMONG the more remarkable Canadian success stories of recent years. In the early 1980s, the national mail service was in a deep fiscal crisis. It continually ran annual deficits of hundreds of millions of dollars, approaching the $1 billion mark, and future prospects for the then government department were bleak.

It was in 1981 that the federal government of the day moved to take the post office out from under its umbrella and make it stand on its own. The aim was to make Canada Post Corporation, as it would be known, its own administrator and the guardian of its own success. Twenty-plus years later, that could not have proved a better decision. As its fiscal year 2000/2001 drew to a close, the corporation posted profits of some $84 million, the sixth consecutive year the corporation had run its margins into the black. In fewer than 20 years, Canada Post had gone from a money-losing government service to a vibrant, multifaceted Crown corporation.

Clockwise from top:
Canada Post's headquarters oversees connections from some 30 million Canadians and 950,000 businesses to each other and to others across the planet.

There are 22 major plants across the country that use high-speed letter-sorting machines, electronic data processors, multiline optical character readers, video encoding systems, and computer-based tracking systems to process billions of pieces of mail each year.

The National Control Centre in Ottawa monitors the movement of mail 24 hours a day, seven days a week, using state-of-the-art technology to ensure Canada Post meets its service standards.

FROM ANYWHERE . . . TO ANYONE

Canada Post's business is, and always has been, about connecting people. Formal postal service was established in Canada in 1763, and message delivery service at that time was based more on the concept of reliably getting a message to someone than it was about offering different solutions for delivery. Gradually, the national mail service began to take on a modern look. Canada Post's predecessor, the Post Office Department, was born in Ottawa on December 21, 1867. During its first year of operation, the department handled more than 20 million letters, 19 million newspapers, and 39,000 parcels.

During the course of its lifetime, Canada Post has been a leading force in international mail delivery. In 1948, Canada was the first country in the world to adopt air carriage of mail. In 1971, Canada furthered that concept by becoming the first country to offer universal airmail

service for international mail. Canada Post joined forces with the U.S. Postal Service and France's La Poste in 1998 to create PosteCS, a secure electronic courier service for documents. In 2000, Canada Post became the first of these three postal administrations to launch PosteCS commercially. In 1999, Canada Post launched epost, the world's first electronic post office.

Perhaps most remarkable of all is that Canada Post has launched all of these innovative new concepts without affecting the price of delivery service. The price of a stamp in Canada in 2001 was the second lowest in the industrialised world, behind Australia. Since 1981, the Canadian consumer price index has risen by 77 percent. The cost of a stamp during that same period rose only 53 percent.

Today, Canada Post offers a wide selection of delivery solutions for both its corporate and its individual clients. Traditional mail delivery remains the cornerstone of all it does, and in 1987, Canada Post was the first postal administration in the world to engage an external auditor to measure its delivery service performance. That study showed that Canada Post was then at a success rate of below 85 percent. Today, on all types of mail, its success rate consistently runs in the high 90s.

Canada Post also offers a range of distribution services–including Priority Courier, Xpresspost, Expedited Parcel, and Regular Parcel. Through its subsidiary company, Purolator Courier, Canada Post is further able to provide fast, reliable package delivery across the country.

Canada Post offers a range of services aside from just physical mail. The corporation's Web site presents a wide variety of services, from postal code look-ups to delivery confirmations. For the business community, Canada Post offers its epost and PosteCS services–secure solutions for electronic bill presentment and electronic couriering, respectively. More than that, it offers solutions for business marketing, mass mailings, shipping, and supply chain management.

MAKING DISTANCES DISAPPEAR

The power of Canada Post is its ability to connect some 30 million Canadians and 950,000 businesses to each other and to others across the planet. Across the country, there are some 936,000 points of entry into Canada's postal system and some 24,000 retail points of access. Canada Post is also a key employer in the country. It is ranked 39th among Canadian businesses in terms of consolidated revenues, and is the sixth-largest employer in the country.

Using high-speed letter-sorting machines, electronic data processors, multiline character readers, video encoding systems, and computer-based tracking systems, Canada Post Corporation's team of some 64,000 employees collects, processes, and delivers nearly 10 billion messages and parcels annually. Of the country's some 13 million addresses, there is none to which Canada Post does not deliver–something that no other delivery service can boast.

There can be no doubt that the face of message delivery is changing rapidly, and with it, postal administrations such as Canada Post face new demands and challenges. The key to remaining successful in the marketplace is to diversify products and service bases–and that is exactly what Canada Post has done in the information age. Customer satisfaction, cost management, and a variety of end-to-end solutions are the cornerstones of Canada Post's business today. It's no longer about simple mail delivery. Today, and into the future, Canada Post is basing its business on connecting people through all means–whether physical, electronic, or a hybrid of both.

A familiar sight across the country, Canada Post's fleet of more than 6,000 vehicles logs more than 74 million kilometres a year.

Some 64,000 Canada Post Corporation employees collect, process, and deliver nearly 10 billion messages and parcels annually.

Canadian Postal Museum, Canadian Museum of Civilization

Located within the confines of Ottawa's National Capital Region in the Canadian Museum of Civilization, the Canadian Postal Museum seeks to enrich the public's knowledge of the long-standing history of postal communication and its evolving role in society throughout the years. The museum offers a collection of hundreds of thousands of philatelic items, as well as works of art, mail carriers' uniforms, letter boxes, and even a restored rural post office.

The 8,500-square-foot Canadian Postal Museum has been a mainstay of the Canadian Museum of Civilization since 1997. Founded in 1971, the museum opened in 1974 and occupied several spaces until it found its current home. Since relocating to the Canadian Museum of Civilization, the Canadian Postal Museum has experienced a more than tenfold increase in attendance and, in 2000, it ranked as the second-best-attended postal museum in the world. Each year, some 300,000 visitors come to the Postal Museum to experience the history and heritage of Canada's postal communications.

The message of the Canadian Postal Museum caters to visitors of all ages, including informative displays that relate the history of postal uniforms, a mock-up of Canada Post's National Control Centre, and the dramatic story of wartime mail. Also, a number of interactive displays encourage youth to learn more about the history of the postal service in Canadian culture. This historical account of the role of the postal service in Canadian society is an educational experience not soon forgotten.

The Canadian Postal Museum, Canadian Museum of Civilization caters to visitors of all ages with displays that relate the history of the postal service. (Clockwise, from top) a participant in the Stamp Quest design contest; the entrance to the Postal museum; a welcome display at the museum's entrance; a brass clock previously located at the Besserer Street post office in Ottawa; and 1908 letter carriers in Kitchener

Claire Dufour

National Archives of Canada

Steven Darby

Postal Heritage in Evolution

While stamps and philatelic rarities certainly play a role in the Canadian Postal Museum's exhibits, the overall scope of the museum is to illustrate the history, heritage, and evolution of postal communications in Canada and around the world. A large display titled *Signed, Sealed, Delivered* highlights the history of postal service and the evolution of the printed word. Other exhibits examine the role of the letter carrier, as well as the role of the evolution of transport and its effect on mail distribution and stamp art. The museum also considers the social role of mail: During wartime, for example, mail was the only means of communication between Canadians at home and loved ones overseas, and for that reason, mail became a significant part of Canadians' daily lives.

The temporary exhibit space regularly features exhibits that explore different facets of postal history. One early exhibit, called *Winged Messenger*, explored the history of air mail, while another exhibit featured Jean Paul Lemieux, a Canadian painter whose works were used in the 1984 Canada Day stamp series. In the future, the Canadian Postal Museum, Canadian Museum of Civilization has plans to include more dynamic exhibits, including one on the evolution of catalogue shopping and another dealing with the post and popular culture.

Ritchie Feed & Seed Inc.

RITCHIE FEED & SEED INC. TRACES ITS OTTAWA ROOTS BACK TO 1930, when Jack Ritchie started the family business that would bear his name more than 70 years later. At that time, the business focussed on agricultural feed, but it wasn't long before the company expanded its operations into other agricultural products and into the retail lawn and garden products market.

In 1960, Ritchie Feed & Seed moved to its current location on Windmill Lane in the east end of the City of Ottawa. In 1982, the firm expanded out into the city's west end with a location in Stittsville. Today, between the two outlets, the company displays a myriad of agricultural and consumer products across more than three acres of space. The Windmill Lane outlet is one of the largest garden centres in the city, spanning more than 16,000 square feet of retail space, and more than two acres of outdoor space. Ritchie Feed & Seed also operates under the banner C & L Feed, serving clients outside of the Ottawa area with two feed outlets in Winchester and Chesterville, and a grist mill in Dixon's Corners.

HIGH-TECH SOLUTIONS FOR FARMERS' NEEDS

Staying true to its roots, Ritchie Feed & Seed continues to conduct the majority of its business as a provider of agricultural products for farmers' needs. In fact, about 60 percent of the firm's business is the supply of products to dairy, beef, hog, and poultry farmers in eastern Ontario, who are constantly looking for the perfect feed that will keep their livestock healthy and strong.

Ritchie Feed & Seed is one of the few agricultural feed suppliers with a laboratory on site. On any given day, a farmer might come into Ritchie's Windmill Lane office with a sample of hay and grain being fed to his cattle. Ritchie's staff will then analyse those samples and, with some additional information provided by the farmer, devise a feed ration that will keep the farmer's livestock healthy. It's a classic example of high technology meeting what has traditionally been considered a low-tech industry.

A WEALTH OF LAWN AND GARDEN SUPPLIES

While the majority of Ritchie's business may come from farmers, the spring and fall planting seasons are a bit like Christmastime at the company's retail stores. The two Ritchie Feed & Seed outlets bustle with customers buying a vast array of lawn and garden supplies, aided by a knowledgeable staff ready to help solve any problems a customer may have. From the city's largest selection of seeds and bulbs to lawn ornaments, sod, trees, shrubs, and flowers, there is little that is not in stock at Ritchie Feed & Seed; there is less still that the company cannot special order for a customer.

While gardening may be a seasonal activity, Ritchie Feed & Seed Inc. operates year-round, although much of its business in the winter months is focussed on agricultural feed. The business has been characterized by steady growth in recent years, and that is something that has company owners optimistic about the future development of Ritchie Feed & Seed, whether in terms of outright expansion or of additional growth.

General Dynamics Canada

I T IS IMPOSSIBLE TO CAPTURE THE INNOVATIVE SPIRIT OF OTTAWA without including companies that have been instrumental in transforming the city into the high-technology capital that it is today. General Dynamics Canada (formerly Computing Devices Canada) is one of those companies. Dipix Technologies Inc., Lumonics Inc., and Neptec Design Group Ltd. are but a few examples of companies that were spun off from General Dynamics Canada after its inception as Computing Devices in 1948.

General Dynamics Canada, with headquarters in Ottawa, is a wholly owned subsidiary of General Dynamics Corporation, which has leading market positions in business aviation, information systems, shipbuilding and marine systems, and land and amphibious combat systems.

The roots of General Dynamics Canada go back to when the Canadian Naval Electrical Laboratory (CNEL) turned to two Polish engineers and their Irish-Canadian business partner to develop a simulator to teach naval tactics. Little did they realize at the time that this initial contract would launch a company that would go from one success to another for more than half a century by developing leading-edge defence technologies.

WORLD FIRSTS AND BUSINESS EXPERTISE

General Dynamics Canada introduced the position and homing indicator in 1952 and the projected map system in 1963, both of which were revolutionary airborne navigational devices in their day. These devices were followed by the first army digital fire control computer in 1973, as well as the world's first fully integrated voice and data military communication system in 1998. Most recently, the company has introduced some of the world's most advanced land mine and biological detection systems.

General Dynamics Canada's engineers, technologists, and support staffs have extensive intellectual capital and business experience. Together, they provide research and development, engineering design, electronics manufacturing, life cycle support, and systems integration activities for General Dynamics Canada's domestic and international customer base. More than 1,500 highly skilled individuals are employed in facilities located in Ottawa, Calgary, and Halifax.

AN INTRINSIC PART OF THE COMMUNITY

As General Dynamics Canada has grown and prospered over the years, the company has always been and will continue to be involved in making Ottawa a great place to live and work. Whether supporting the United Way Campaign, the educational partnership with Bell High School, the Pioneers Association, or Queensway-Carleton hospital – to which General Dynamics Canada has made very significant contributions – the company has long and deep roots in the community.

AIRBORNE, MARITIME, AND VETRONICS SYSTEMS

General Dynamics Canada's Airborne Systems has more than 35 years of experience in the design, engineering development, production, and field support of airborne equipment. Recognized as a world leader in airborne acoustic applications, the company has acquired the knowledge, skills, and experience necessary to successfully pursue major systems integration programs such as Canada's Maritime Helicopter Project.

With more than 40 years experience in undersea warfare and system integration, the company's Maritime Systems division provides integrated solutions for shipborne and shorebased applications. Over the years, General Dynamics Canada's development of high-fidelity acoustic processors and simulators has contributed both to the company's growth and to recent major achievements in data fusion and multisensor integration.

The company introduced the projected map system in 1963, which was a revolutionary airborne navigational device in its day.

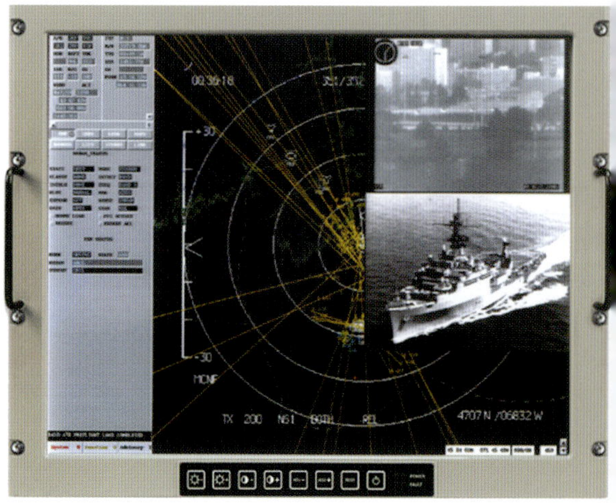

laritime Systems is active within
anada and abroad, supporting at-sea
apabilities, developing next-generation
olutions, and successfully competing in
demanding worldwide market.

ieneral Dynamics Canada developed
ne world's first fully digitized ballistic
omputer system in the late 1970s for
ne U.S. Army's M1A1 Abrams
nain battle tank. Today, the digital
re control system has been integrated
nto battle management systems
hat incorporate the functions of
re control, situational awareness
nd target detection and recognition,
s well as presenting correlated in-
ormation to the crew on common
isplay devices.

A pioneer in the application of digital electronics, General Dynamics Canada offers integrated solutions across the digitized battlespace.

OMMAND CONTROL, COMMUNICATIONS ND INTEGRATED SENSOR SYSTEMS

ieneral Dynamics Canada continues
o lead the way in battlefield digiti-
ation with the successful development,
ntegration, and deployment of the
vorld's first fully digitized military
ommunications system to the
anadian Army. Building on this
xperience and accrued engineering
kills, the company won the $4 billion
J.K. Bowman communications system
n the face of strong international
ompetition making it the largest
efence export in Canadian history.

ieneral Dynamics Canada, is a
vholly owned subsidiary of General
Dynamics Corporation, headquartered
n Falls Church, Virginia, which
mploys approximately 54,000
eople. The company has leading
narket positions in business aviation,
nformation systems, shipbuilding
nd marine systems, and land and
mphibious combat systems.

General Dynamics Canada's engineers, technologists, and support staffs provide research and development, engineering design, electronics manufacturing, life cycle support, and systems integration for the company's domestic and international customer base.

Daoust Construction

Paul Daoust started Daoust Construction, established in Ottawa in 1952, with the aim of continuing the traditions of excellence that his father, Eugene–a builder and owner of a lumber company–and grandfather Joseph–a carpenter–started. Paul's objective and mission was to continue the family tradition of trust, excellence, quality work, and a fundamental pride in service–values that today are still at the core of all that Daoust Construction does.

Today, the fourth generation of Daousts continues the tradition. Jean and Pierre, Paul's sons, manage the business with the same commitments that their father embodied. The historic traits of quality work, ethical business practices, and teamwork remain at the foundation of Daoust Construction's mission, and they are the cornerstones upon which the company's reputation rests.

Quality Work and Quality Management

The 50-plus-year history of the company has seen Daoust Construction and the industry in which it works change significantly. When Paul Daoust first began business, quality work hinged on quality materials and workmanship–the more tangible aspects of a construction project. Today, the world of Jean and Pierre Daoust hinges as much on quality work as it does on the quality of the management services the team provides to its clients. That goes beyond simply delivering a quality project on time and within budget–although those concepts certainly remain paramount; the concept of quality work also extends to providing excellence in service to achieve a project's goals and a client's needs.

The construction services that Daoust Construction provides are professional services, relying on the highest level of dedication to central concepts such as teamwork and putting the owner's interests at the front of every decision. To that end, Daoust Construction offers a number of project delivery methods, including program management (planning), project management (leadership), design build, and general contracting.

Apart from all of these factors is the firm's signature method of construction management (execution), a project delivery method that has helped set Daoust Construction apart from the pack and is the method of choice for the company and its clients.

The Collective Effort

Using its construction management method, Daoust Construction works in partnership with the owner and the design team to deliver the best value project in the shortest possible time. This process makes for a superior-built final product, and one in which the time and cost elements are used to their fullest potential. In conjunction with leading architects, engineers, and owners across Ottawa and throughout Ontario, Quebec, the Nunavut Territories, and Florida, Daoust Construction remains a leader in building facilities for the industrial, commercial, institutional and even multiresidential markets. Daoust Construction's project track record and experienced professional staff allow the company to deliver a successful, high-quality project using any of its project delivery methods available in any geographic region.

Daoust Construction worked in conjunction with leading architects, engineers, and owners in Ottawa for the University of Ottawa's School of Information and Technology Engineering (top) and in Orlando, Florida, on the Point Orlando retail and entertainment complex (bottom right). Information on the company and the work it has done can be found on its Web site, www.dc.ca.

Daoust Construction offers a professional, proactive, hands on team approach to its clients (bottom left).

Coughlin & Associates Ltd.

JAMES E. COUGHLIN FOUNDED COUGHLIN & ASSOCIATES LTD. IN Ottawa in 1958. In its early days, the firm's goal was based as much on survival as it was on keeping customers satisfied. Its principal clientele was multi-employer organizations, like construction trade unions and some associations. Specializing in employee benefits, the company tailors group benefits packages for employees of all different types of companies and organizations.

Much has changed in the decades since Coughlin & Associates Ltd.'s inception. Michel Poirier is the firm's third president, having assumed that role in 1984. He succeeded Reginald Gill, who, in turn, ran operations after Coughlin himself retired as president in 1980. Though headquartered in Ottawa, the range of the company's operations spans the entire country. The firm's Winnipeg office, established in 1965, manages affairs in the Prairie Provinces, while the head office manages operations in British Columbia, Ontario, Quebec, and the Maritimes.

COUGHLIN & ASSOCIATES LTD. IS LOCATED IN THE ATTRACTIVE, CONVENIENTLY LOCATED SAKTO COMPLEX ON PRESTON STREET NEAR THE HEART OF THE NATION'S CAPITAL.

While most of Coughlin & Associates Ltd.'s clients remain from the initial years, the firm has diversified itself by providing services to clients in various sectors. Ottawa's high-technology sector is one group of employers who have recently come to use the expertise of Coughlin & Associates Ltd.

EXPERTISE IN ACTION

Coughlin & Associates Ltd. takes a unique, two-pronged approach. Unlike its competitors, the firm manages both sides of employee benefit programs: consultancy and administration. The company's consulting division works with firms to design and implement the best possible benefits program. That means consultants from Coughlin & Associates Ltd. work one-on-one with corporate clients to determine the goals of the program, the plan requirements, and how these requirements should be implemented.

THE COUGHLIN & ASSOCIATES LTD. EXECUTIVE TEAM IS MADE UP OF (FROM LEFT) MARK HOGAN, ASSOCIATE VICE-PRESIDENT; KIRBY WATSON, VICE-PRESIDENT, WESTERN CANADA; MICHEL POIRIER, PRESIDENT; AND BRIAN BOCKSTAEL, VICE-PRESIDENT, EASTERN CANADA.

But Coughlin & Associates Ltd.'s role does not end there. The firm also administers the plan for its clients, acting as insurers' representatives. If an employee must make a claim under his or her benefit plan, he or she can mail or fax the claim to Coughlin & Associates Ltd. and get the refund within days.

What's more, the firm adds a personal element to the realm of insurance claims. Often, insurance carriers will discourage individual clients from coming to their offices to process claims, preferring instead a mailed-in claim form, or one submitted electronically. Not so at Coughlin & Associates Ltd. On any given day, individual clients can be found completing claims forms in the firm's front lobby processing area.

In fact, Poirier says, it's not uncommon to see as many as 200 clients each day coming into the office with claims. Most walk-in claims are processed in fewer than 30 minutes. "For many people, the $200 or $300 they spend at the dentist is a lot of money to be without," says Poirier. "That can be a hardship, so we try to make sure that walk-in clients get their money within 30 minutes or less."

From individual financial services, to managed health care services, to pension plans, registered retirement savings plans (RRSP), registered retirement income funds (RRIF), and life insurance, Coughlin & Associates Ltd. offers the full range of benefits packages for its clients, all with a commitment to serving clients in the best possible manner.

SERVICE BEYOND EXPECTATIONS™

The service standard of a 48-hour turnaround on claims is just one example of the benchmarks that Coughlin & Associates Ltd. sets for itself. The corporate motto, printed on all employees' business cards, is Service Beyond Expectations. That begins with the two-pronged approach to benefits package planning and extends from conducting information sessions for the plan's end users to processing claims.

Coughlin & Associates Ltd.'s service philosophy is backed by state-of-the-art information systems (left).

Coughlin's consultants analyse and design employee benefits programs, as well as communicate individually with employees and members to address benefits inquiries, host seminars, develop communications, and establish processes to ensure benefits meet the long-term needs of plan sponsors and members (right).

'oirier says that the main problem nost employees have with their enefits package is a lack of infornation. Most people do not take he time to research what their enefits package covers, and that an lead to major problems when t comes time to complete a claim. With that in mind, the company ncourages its corporate clients to rrange special information sessions or their employees, hosted by repesentatives from Coughlin & Assoiates Ltd., who outline the specifics of their packages.

Through these information sessions nd regular meetings with clients, Coughlin & Associates Ltd.'s consultnts can get a sense of how well ackages work, and identify and orrect any potential problems.

"Clients invest a lot of money in their benefits packages, and we want to make sure that they get the bang for their buck," says Poirier. "It's important that their employees understand the structure of their benefits package."

A PART OF THE COMMUNITY

Coughlin & Associates Ltd. has also taken to heart the principle of giving back to the community of which it has been a part for more than 40 years. The company is a member of the national Imagine program—a program created by the Canadian Centre for Philanthropy to recognize those corporate bodies who give more than one percent of their annual pretax income to charity. Coughlin & Associates Ltd. exceeds that minimum figure by making donations to the Boys & Girls Club of Ottawa-Carleton, Juvenile Diabetes Association, United Way, Ottawa Hospital Foundation, and many other causes. Employees also volunteer their own time to support these and other causes.

Coughlin & Associates Ltd. has been a good corporate citizen, and the firm's commitment to Service Beyond Expectations has enabled it to create a niche for itself in the marketplace. Through its unique approach to creating and administering employee benefit programs, the company has become one of the leading firms in the field of employee benefits. And the end result has been a host of satisfied customers in Ottawa and throughout Canada.

Service Beyond Expectations™ is the core philosophy of Coughlin & Associates Ltd. Claims adjudicators assess and process health and dental claims while the customer waits, usually in less than 30 minutes, and other claims are processed and reimbursed within days—compared to weeks or even months by other providers (left).

Training, teamwork, and peer review form a key part of Coughlin & Associates Ltd.'s commitment to providing Service Beyond Expectations™ (right).

Southway Inn of Ottawa

From a humble beginning, Southway Inn of Ottawa, built some 45 years ago as a seven-room motel, has grown into a mighty Ottawa presence. Today, Southway Inn's 170 rooms make it one of the larger independently owned hotels in Ottawa, as well as one of the more popular destinations for tourists who come looking for the high standard of customer service that Peter and Theresia Zlepnig introduced to the city in 1958.

Southway Inn of Ottawa's 170 rooms make it one of the larger independently owned hotels in Ottawa and a popular tourist destination.

In 1958, the Zlepnigs purchased a 10-acre tract of land at what was then the southernmost end of Bank Street. They built a seven-unit motel and a modest family home on the property, and thus Southway Inn was born. Clientele in those days consisted mostly of airline crews and tourists who chose Southway Inn because of its proximity to the airport, which was separated from the inn by woodlots and farmers' fields. It would be another 30 years before the area around the hotel began to turn into the bustling part of Ottawa that it is today.

As demand grew, so did Southway Inn; the small hotel increased by 13 units in its first five years of operation. In 1960, the Zlepnig family attached three more rooms to their family home to accommodate more guests, raising capacity to 23 rooms. When Peter passed away in 1962, the Zlepnigs' son, Bill, came on board to work with Theresia in the family's hotel.

In 1984, the area around Southway Inn began to develop, and Bill Zlepnig decided that the hotel must grow with it. That year, Southway Inn was rebuilt; the existing, 23-room property, which had served as home to the Zlepnig family for so long, was razed, with a new, two-storey, 57-unit building taking its place. In 1988, the family expanded the hotel further, this time adding another storey and 45 more rooms. Thereafter, Southway Inn featured an indoor swimming pool, a recreation complex, and two meeting rooms.

Also in 1984, the Zlepnig family assumed control of the Shallows, the full-service restaurant located on site. Today, the Shallows continues to offer traditional fare at a reasonable price, and has become a destination for diners in the city, as well as for hotel guests, with its live music and prime rib specials.

An Oasis in the Heart of Ottawa

Today, the third generation of the Zlepnig family is at the helm of Southway Inn. Bill Zlepnig continues to serve in an official capacity at the hotel as its president, and was instrumental in planning the most recent addition to the hotel—another 75 rooms—which was completed in November 2001. Bill's wife, Louisa, is Vice-President, and their children—Stephen, who serves as General Manager; Linda, who is Office Manager/Human Resources Man-

Common facilities at the hotel include seven meeting rooms, all with access to the Internet, fax machines, telephones, and photocopiers; an athletics room; an indoor swimming pool; and an outdoor courtyard.

ager; and Fred, who serves as Director of the company–all play active roles in the daily affairs of the family business.

Though still drawing business from the airport, Southway Inn now counts as part of its clientele a good number of technology professionals who come to Ottawa on business. For this reason, the hotel has made its atmosphere as accommodating to the business traveller as it has to the tourist. All rooms are oversize and equipped with high-speed Internet access, digital phone lines, and caller identification, as well as 27-inch televisions. Common facilities at the hotel include seven meeting rooms, all with access to the Internet, fax machines, telephones, and photocopiers; an athletics room; an indoor swimming pool; and an outdoor courtyard.

"The city is growing and its needs are changing," explains Stephen Zlepnig. "Because of that, we have to change to meet our guests' needs. Since this is a smaller hotel, we're able to be more responsive and more flexible."

As the hospitality industry, like so many others, undergoes a process of consolidation and amalgamation, an independently run hotel rarely stays successful for a long period of time unless it offers something to make its services stand out. Managers of larger hotels have approached Stephen Zlepnig and spoken of Southway Inn's influence on their bigger properties. While many of the larger hotels are better known than Southway Inn, there is a service standard that exists at the hotel that its competitors have difficulty matching.

FAMILY TREATMENT

The Zlepnigs take pride in their ability to serve their guests in the best possible manner. In the early 1950s, Theresia Zlepnig used to provide guests with meals at Christmas and other treats. Today, guests continue to be treated like family, and the hotel's staff members strive to make Southway Inn a home away from home for all travellers. Proof of their success is shown through the number of repeat guests and the comment cards that sing the praises of Southway Inn.

Down the road, Stephen Zlepnig says he would like to see Southway Inn of Ottawa expand, perhaps to another city. Since guests often ask if there is a Southway Inn in other places, he says expansion could work. However, the emphasis will continue to be on the quality of service the hotel has offered. Says Zlepnig, "Always, we will make the commitment to continue the family legacy of impeccable service."

All rooms are oversize and equipped with high-speed Internet access, digital phone lines, and caller identification, as well as 27-inch televisions.

At Southway Inn there is a service standard that exists that the hotel's competitors have difficulty matching.

Tommy & Lefebvre

ASK ANY EMPLOYEE AT TOMMY & LEFEBVRE WHAT SETS THE COMPANY apart from the other sporting goods retailers across Ottawa and they'll tell you there is a passion for sports that runs among all of the company's some 300 employees. Whether the sport is golfing, skiing, biking, inline skating, or snow boarding, each employee is active in some way in at least one such pursuit. For the customers at each one of the chain's stores, that means expert product advice from people who know what works and what doesn't.

Tommy & Lefebvre has embodied a passion for sports since its inception. Brothers Art and Andy Tommy partnered with Reg Lefebvre to start the retail company in 1958. They started humbly, selling ski equipment during the winter months and boats and other watercraft during the summer. A steady growth over the years has led to six locations and a reputation for quality, brand-name merchandise.

THE TOMMY & LEFEBVRE EXECUTIVE TEAM CONSISTS OF (FROM LEFT) FRED TOMMY, COMPTROLLER; NATALIE TOMMY, VICE-PRESIDENT; AND KEVIN PIDGEON, PRESIDENT.

After the passing of Art Tommy and Reg Lefebvre, company president Kevin Pidgeon decided to evolve Tommy & Lefebvre from a winter-driven business to more well-rounded one with golf, bike, and inline contributing equally. That year, the firm began to entrench the market, and Pidgeon credits good timing and a rise in the sport's popularity as helping to make golf equipment one of the largest components of Tommy & Lefebvre's sales today. The store now offers a wide selection of ski, golf, bike, snow board, and inline skate equipment, as well as active wear.

Today, Pidgeon says that if Tommy & Lefebvre is not among the top three retailers in any field within five years of adopting a product line, the company will abandon it. "We want to be trendsetters in any field, and above all, we want to be as much help to our customers as possible," says Pidgeon. "Our job is about improving their performance on the slopes or on the course, and we want to make sure that every customer has the right product for his or her needs. That's why we're involved with sports–so we can give the most value to the participants."

THE MAIN LOCATION FOR TOMMY & LEFEBVRE IS ON BANK STREET.

JOHN HENRY PHOTO

Pidgeon assumed control of the company's operations when Reg Lefebvre and Art Tommy died in 1993 and 1994, respectively. Natalie Tommy–Pidgeon's wife and Art Tommy's daughter–and Art and Andy's brother Fred have assisted in running the business with the same commitment to the business and passion for all things sporting that Art Tommy personified.

A DIFFERENT LEVEL OF SERVICE

Being committed to the products the company sells goes beyond simply loving sports. Each of Tommy & Lefebvre's employees is sent to the company's training camp before starting work on the floor. There, he or she spends more than 360 hours learning about the latest in industry trends and service methods. In addition, manufacturers' representatives often visit the Tommy & Lefebvre head office to train new staff, and all new employees are required to pass product-knowledge tests.

ENTHUSIASTIC CUSTOMER SERVICE SPECIALISTS ARE SENT TO THE COMPANY'S TRAINING CAMP BEFORE STARTING WORK ON THE FLOOR (LEFT).

TOMMY & LEFEBVRE HAS BUILT ITS REPUTATION ON EXCELLENT CUSTOMER SERVICE (RIGHT).

Tommy & Lefebvre operates five stores across the city of Ottawa. The head office is on Bank Street, and four satellite stores are located in Kanata, Orleans, Gatineau, and on Carling Avenue. It's the local aspect of the service that Tommy & Lefebvre provides that also helps set the company apart from its competitors, and for that reason, Pidgeon says he has no plans to expand outside of Ottawa.

"Since we are locally run, we are better able to serve our customers," says Natalie Tommy. "We can respond faster to their needs and order different products for each store, depending on their particular market needs. We also offer one of the best, most liberal return policies in the industry. If a customer doesn't like a product for any reason, he or she can return it to us, with no questions asked." She adds that Tommy & Lefebvre has the largest selection of ski and snow board products in eastern Canada, and the company is always able to offer the best prices.

COMMITTED TO THE SPORTING COMMUNITY

Athleticism runs throughout the Tommy family. Natalie speaks of grandfathers and a brother who played football professionally in the Canadian Football League, while her father and uncle founded the Canadian national ski team. The family is proud of its roots, and knows that the sports field is a tough area in which to compete and excel. Even tougher for some is the financial burden that comes with playing competitively. For that reason, Tommy & Lefebvre has made a commitment to funding, whenever it can, amateur athletes who could not otherwise afford to finance their passion.

Each year, the Art Tommy Memorial Foundation gives out $10,000 to $20,000 in donations to local alpine racers who have the talent, but might not otherwise have the money to fund their love of competition. That money can go to purchasing equipment or paying for accommodations at a race–anything an athlete needs to fuel his or her dream.

On top of that, the company also sponsors many local charitable events that benefit amateur sports. On race day, Tommy & Lefebvre will sponsor or donate prizes, or the company will host evenings in support of young skiers. During the summer months, the firm is also involved with promoting local golfers. It's all about giving back to the sporting community and participating whenever the company can at all levels.

"You have to have a love of sports to be in this business," says Natalie Tommy. "This is not just a workplace for us. We love this environment, and we love working with people. I think that shows through in all that we do."

▶ JOHN HENRY PHOTO

FRIENDLY SERVICE AND UNBEATABLE SELECTION ARE TOMMY & LEFEBVRE HALLMARKS.

National Capital Commission

In the early 1800s, the area that is now the National Capital Region was an industrial town choked with railways, factories, and lumber mills. Bytown was founded in 1826 at the point where the Ottawa and Rideau rivers meet and was renamed Ottawa in 1855. By 1857, it had become the capital of the new Province of Canada, and when the Dominion of Canada celebrated Confederation in 1867, Ottawa became the new capital of Canada.

In 1899, Parliament created the Ottawa Improvement Commission (OIC) to beautify the capital, and 1927 saw the OIC evolve into the larger Federal District Commission, whose focus was "to work for the general advantage of Canada." This later gave way to the National Capital Commission (NCC) in 1959.

Parliament gave the NCC a mandate to undertake "the development, conservation, and improvement of the National Capital Region" so that the capital would properly represent Canada as it grew into a great modern nation. That mandate was expanded in 1988 to include increased emphasis on the NCC's role as an organizer and coordinator of national celebrations and public events.

When the first general plan for the Ottawa area was sketched out, there was a sense that Canada's capital–if it was really to represent the country–should be a "green" capital. Certainly, the landscape around the capital had extraordinary natural potential. With the ancient rocks of the Canadian Shield bordering the region to the north and a rich river valley spreading out to the south, the area has always boasted a broad array of vegetation and wildlife. In the past century, the NCC and its forerunners have built on this natural richness–not only beautifying the capital and gradually changing it from a wilderness outpost into a modern metropolis, but also creating a national capital that reflects all Canadians.

Fulfilling Its Mandate

The NCC's mandate, simply put, is to plan, develop, and use the capital region as a source of pride and unity for Canadians.

As the steward of federal lands and buildings in Canada's capital region, the NCC today owns 465 square kilometres of land in the capital region (nearly 10 percent of the whole), and is responsible for maintaining a variety of properties. Many Canadians–both at the NCC and from across Canada–have contributed their time and expertise to

The National Capital Commission (NCC) was given a mandate by Parliament to undertake "the development, conservation, and improvement of the National Capital Region" so that the capital would properly represent Canada as it grew into a great modern nation.

The NCC has protected more than 50,000 hectares of conservation land, parks, and green spaces and constructed hundreds of kilometres of roads.

create a series of plans that guide the ownership, management, development, and use of federal lands in the capital region.

Along with planning, NCC experts are also involved in designing, building, maintaining, and preserving federal assets in the capital region. Over the past century, the NCC, its predecessors, and its partners have built up an impressive list of accomplishments. They constructed six major bridges and hundreds of kilometres of roads; protected more than 50,000 hectares of conservation land, parks, and green spaces, including Gatineau Park and the Greenbelt; created large expanses of urban parks and connecting green spaces; and bought and saved many heritage buildings and other capital treasures from destruction. They also built the Capital Pathway, one of the most extensive recreational pathway networks in North America; developed Confederation Boulevard, a ceremonial route that links the Ontario and Quebec sides of the National Capital Region; and helped the capital region evolve into a city of scenic parkways and waterside parks, where nature and the environment exist in harmony.

The NCC works with partners to animate the capital as well. It organizes national celebrations for Canadians and promotes activities

The NCC organizes national celebrations for Canadians and promotes activities and events that reflect Canadians in their diversity.

and events that reflect Canadians in their diversity. Examples of animation in the capital region include programs and infrastructure in natural areas, such as interpretation panels, boardwalks, and educational activities; the Canada and the World Pavilion, where Canadian achievements on the international stage are celebrated; and seasonal festivals and celebrations.

A CAPITAL FOR CANADIANS

The work of the NCC translates into a quality of life that residents and visitors can enjoy throughout the capital region all year long. Fall Rhapsody draws people from far and wide to experience the brilliant colours of Gatineau Park. In December, the Christmas Lights Across Canada program celebrates the holiday season with thousands of colourful lights along Confederation Boulevard, and symbolically links all Canadian capitals. The first three weekends of February bring some 1.6 million visits to Winterlude, one of North America's greatest winter festivals. In the spring, Canadians converge on the capital to see more than a million tulips brighten the NCC flower beds during the Canadian Tulip Festival. And on July 1, more than 350,000 people rally in the streets of the capital for the country's birthday and Canada's biggest party of the year.

Along with special events, the NCC also contributes to simple, everyday pleasures in the capital as well—hiking up to Gatineau Park's Champlain Lookout for a fantastic view, feeding a chickadee, or listening to a whole symphony of birds in the Greenbelt. The thrill of racing down the world's longest skating rink on a pair of newly sharpened skates. The fun of exploring the capital on foot and posing for a photograph beside a public art piece on the bank of the Rideau Canal.

Canada's capital region boasts a diverse, vibrant, and creative community, a community that reflects Canadians as the capital reflects Canada. The NCC is proud to contribute to the quality of life for Canadians in the capital.

THE WORK OF THE NCC TRANSLATES INTO A QUALITY OF LIFE THAT RESIDENTS AND VISITORS CAN ENJOY THROUGHOUT THE CAPITAL REGION ALL YEAR LONG.

Commission de la capitale nationale

Au début du 18e siècle, la région de la capitale nationale est une ville industrielle étouffée par les voies ferrées, les usines et les scieries. En 1826, la ville de Bytown voit le jour au confluent des rivières des Outaouais et Rideau. Deux ans après avoir été rebaptisée Ottawa, soit en 1857, elle devient la capitale de la nouvelle province du Canada. Au moment des célébrations de la Confédération en 1867, Ottawa devient la capitale d'un nouveau pays : le Canada.

En 1899, le Parlement crée la Commission d'amélioration d'Ottawa (CAO) afin d'embellir la capitale. La CAO devient, en 1927, la Commission du district fédéral (CDF) élargie ayant la responsabilité « de travailler pour le bien général du Canada ». La CDF devient par la suite la Commission de la capitale nationale (CCN) en 1959.

Le Parlement donne alors le mandat à la CCN d'entreprendre « l'aménagement, la conservation et l'embellissement de la région de la capitale nationale » de sorte que la capitale représente dignement le Canada, qui allait devenir un grand pays moderne. En 1988, ce mandat a été élargi, et la CCN a maintenant aussi comme fonction d'organiser et de coordonner des célébrations nationales et des activités publiques.

Le premier grand plan pour la région d'Ottawa a été rédigé avec le sentiment que la capitale du Canada – pour bien représenter le pays – devrait être « verte ». Il n'y a pas de doute que la capitale, vu le paysage qui l'entoure, a beaucoup à offrir sur le plan de la nature. Les anciennes pierres du Bouclier canadien bordent la limite nord de la région, et une riche vallée fluviale s'étend vers le sud; au centre, la région a toujours montré une végétation abondante et une faune diversifiée. Au cours du dernier siècle, la CCN et ses prédécesseurs ont façonné cette richesse naturelle – non seulement ont-ils embelli la capitale et transformé le poste sauvage qu'était la région au début du siècle en une grande ville moderne, mais ils ont aussi réussi à créer une capitale nationale à l'image de tous les Canadiens.

Au cours du dernier siècle, les réalisations de la CCN, des organismes qui l'ont précédée et de ses partenaires sont impressionnantes. On n'a qu'à penser à la construction d'une demi-douzaine de ponts d'envergure et des centaines de kilomètres de routes.

La CCN contribue également aux joies de la vie quotidienne. Quoi de mieux que de sauter dans une paire de patins fraîchement affûtés afin de patiner sur la plus longue patinoire du monde.

REMPLIR SON MANDAT

Le mandat de la CCN consiste à planifier, à aménager et à utiliser la région de la capitale afin qu'elle suscite fierté et unité chez les Canadiens.

À titre de protecteur des terrains et des édifices fédéraux de la région de la capitale du Canada, la CCN est aujourd'hui propriétaire de 465 kilomètres carrés de terrains dans la région de la capitale (près de 10 pour cent de l'ensemble du territoire). La CCN est de plus responsable de l'entretien d'une multitude de propriétés. Plusieurs Canadiens – à la CCN et ailleurs au Canada – ont contribué, en donnant de leur temps et en fournissant leur expertise, à la rédaction d'une série de plans visant à guider la possession, la

AU COURS DES TROIS PREMIÈRES FINS DE SEMAINE DE FÉVRIER, BAL DE NEIGE, L'UN DES PLUS GRANDS FESTIVALS D'HIVER EN AMÉRIQUE DU NORD, PROPOSE DES ACTIVITÉS DIVERTISSANTES AUX PETITS COMME AUX GRANDS.

gestion, l'aménagement et l'utilisation des terrains fédéraux dans la région de la capitale.

Les experts de la CCN ne participent pas qu'à la planification, ils travaillent également à l'aménagement, à la construction, à l'entretien et à la conservation de biens fédéraux dans la région de la capitale nationale. Au cours du dernier siècle, les réalisations de la CCN, des organismes qui l'ont précédée et de ses partenaires sont impressionnantes. On n'a qu'à penser à la construction d'une demi-douzaine de ponts d'envergure et de centaines de kilomètres de routes; à la protection de plus de 50 000 hectares de terres protégées, de parcs et d'espaces verts, y compris le parc de la Gatineau et la Ceinture de verdure; à la création de vastes étendues de parcs urbains et d'espaces verts les reliant et à l'achat de plusieurs bâtiments patrimoniaux et d'autres trésors de la capitale afin d'empêcher qu'ils ne soient démolis. On ne saurait passer également sous silence, la construction du Sentier de la capitale, l'un des réseaux de sentiers récréatifs les plus vastes en Amérique du Nord; la création du boulevard de la Confédération, un parcours d'honneur reliant les rives ontariennes et québécoises de la région de la capitale nationale et la contribution visant à faire de la région de la capitale une ville de promenades panoramiques et de parcs au bord de l'eau où la nature et l'environnement cohabitent en harmonie.

La CCN travaille en étroite collaboration avec ses partenaires dans le but d'animer la région de la capitale nationale. La CCN organise des célébrations nationales et fait la promotion d'activités et d'événements démontrant la diversité canadienne. Les programmes et l'infrastructure en milieu naturel comme les panneaux d'interprétation, les passerelles et les activités éducatives; le Pavillon Canada-Monde, lieu par excellence pour souligner les réalisations canadiennes sur la scène internationale, et les célébrations et les festivals saisonniers ne sont que quelques exemples d'animation dan la région de la capitale nationale.

LA COMMISSION DE LA CAPITALE NATIONALE OEUVRE À LA PROTECTION DE PLUS DE 50 000 HECTARES DE TERRES PROTÉGÉES, DE PARCS ET D'ESPACES VERTS.

UNE CAPITALE POUR TOUS LES CANADIENS

Les résidents de la région et les visiteurs profitent du travail de la CCN pendant toute l'année. Le Coloris automnal attire des gens de partout désirant admirer les couleurs éclatantes du parc de la Gatineau. En décembre, les milliers de lumières colorées qui sont installées le long du boulevard de la Confédération, dans le cadre du programme Les lumières de Noël au Canada, permettent de célébrer le temps des Fêtes, et de lier de manière symbolique, toutes les capitales des provinces canadiennes. Au cours des trois premières fins de semaine de février, Bal de Neige, l'un des plus grands festivals d'hiver en Amérique du Nord, enregistre près de 1,6 million de visites. Au printemps, les Canadiens se donnent rendez-vous au Festival canadien des tulipes afin d'assister à l'éclosion d'un million de tulipes venant égayer les platesbandes de la CCN. Le 1er juillet, ce sont plus de 350 000 personnes qui défilent dans les rues de la capitale afin de célébrer la fête du Canada et de participer ainsi à la plus grande fête de l'année au Canada.

La CCN contribue également aux joies de la vie quotidienne. Effectuer une randonnée jusqu'au belvédère Champlain du parc de la Gatineau afin de contempler la vue magnifique; nourrir une mésange à tête noire ou écouter une symphonie d'oiseaux dans la Ceinture de verdure; sauter dans une paire de patins fraîchement affûtés afin de vivre les sensations fortes d'une course sur la plus longue patinoire du monde et goûter au plaisir d'explorer la capitale à pied ou de poser pour un photographe près d'une oeuvre d'art qui orne les lieux publics le long du canal Rideau, voilà autant de petits bonheurs signés CCN.

La région de la capitale du Canada s'enorgueillit de sa communauté diversifiée, vivante et créatrice; une communauté et une capitale à l'image du Canada. La CCN est fière de contribuer à la qualité de vie des Canadiens dans la capitale.

Interactive Circuits and Systems Ltd.

In 1980, Interactive Circuits and Systems Ltd. (ICS) was incorporated by Dr. Dipak Roy and Pierre Ménard. Before then, Ottawa's high-technology community was composed of little more than a handful of companies, many of them working with traditional telephony systems. Popular development of the Internet was years away, and the city's main industry continued to be the federal government, as it had been for some 30 years. Both graduates of Carleton University, Roy and Ménard today represent the elite group of early pioneers who helped shape the high-tech landscape of Ottawa, and ICS is now a global leader in the embedded computer systems industry.

Given the technical background of the principals, ICS' mandate from the very start was to serve the high-end sensor processing markets–sonar, radar, communications, and instrumentation–with high-performance data acquisition and digital signal processing (DSP) products.

MIV PHOTOGRAPHY

Dr. Dipak Roy, Founder and President of Interactive Circuits and Systems Ltd. (ICS) (left)

Pierre Ménard, Founder and Vice-President (right)

THE NECESSARY EXPERIENCE AND KNOWLEDGE

From the basement of a warehouse building, the two ICS principals set out to build their dreams. It was never their intent to solicit outside funds, and their hard work and personal sacrifices were taken for granted. Through untiring and determined efforts, ICS was able to secure–within a short period of time–many small but key developmental contracts from a number of government agencies. The contracts not only enhanced the company's development and credibility, but also provided the necessary experience and knowledge to build complex electronic systems in a multitude of applications.

The company's first major break came in 1986, when ICS won a million-dollar contract from the NATO Saclant Undersea Research Centre in La Spezia, Italy, to supply sonar

MIV PHOTOGRAPHY

ICS' research and development capabilities extend from sonar to cellular.

ICS offers board- and system-level solutions for both military and commercial applications.

ignal processing equipment for both hip- and shore-based installations. CS beat out major European and American defence giants to win this ontract. The success of the contract placed ICS among the premier group of companies with the capability to deliver state-of-the-art signal processing equipment for navy applications.

CS began to grow rapidly, winning more and more contracts with the U.S. Navy. By the early 1990s, the company had become a recognized player in the military sonar market. It was, however, apparent to the ICS management that, for continued growth of revenues and margins, the company had to move more toward standard rather than custom products. The timing could not have been better: in 1994, the U.S. Department of Defense's official procurement policy shifted toward commercial, off-the-shelf (COTS) equipment.

A FAMILY OF PRODUCTS

ICS was ready with a family of dual-use open architecture products that quickly got designed into many major sonar upgrade programs. Notable among them is the SQQ-89 sonar upgrade program for the guided missile (DDG) class of destroyers. This program involves a large number of vessels, and the ICS content is more than $50 million through the life of this program. Other major contracts include the sonar for the New Attack Submarine (NSSN), P3 Aircraft, and radar for the Sea Sparrow missiles.

As ICS continued to develop more and more building block products for sonar, radar, and communications applications, it became apparent that a simple scheme for data flow management was required for rapid system development. Rapid deployment of complex systems is the most effective way to combat the ever-changing threat scenario. In 1995, ICS pioneered the front panel data port (FPDP) data flow concept, working relentlessly to standardize FPDP and lobby the industry partners to incorporate FPDP into their products. In 1999, FPDP became an American National Standards Institute (ANSI) standard, and ICS received a major industry award for its pioneering contribution.

Also in 1999, ICS embarked on a major diversification strategy. The company began developing products that take advantage of the increasing computing power and declining cost of desktop personal computers for the commercial marketplace. The company went through a period of major cultural change that saw it mature into a volume supplier of standard products to both military and commercial markets. The wireless communications and test and measurement applications are the two major commercial areas in which ICS now enjoys significant success.

ICS TODAY AND BEYOND

At the end of the 2001 fiscal year, ICS revenues were approaching $20 million, with commercial sales accounting for close to 30 percent of the total. ICS currently employs more than 50 highly skilled professionals at its facility. ICS America, Inc., a fully owned subsidiary of ICS, is headquartered in Middletown, Rhode Island, with a sales office in California.

Employee satisfaction has been a major factor behind ICS' steady growth. Open access to information and to people, along with rewards for personal and corporate achievements, is the cornerstone of ICS' employment policy. Today, more than two decades following its start, ICS continues to grow, using the vision of its founders, who believed in honesty, integrity, customer service, and technical excellence.

Over the years, Interactive Circuits and Systems Ltd. has developed a rare technical expertise in mixed-signal board design and embedded systems that will help the firm expand, particularly in the commercial marketplace. ICS proudly states that its strength lies in delivering solutions that are exceptionally well engineered, reducing development time for any system that uses its products. From sonar to cellular, ICS' building block boards and systems are the cornerstone for next-generation systems.

MIV PHOTOGRAPHY

PRODUCTION TEST FACILITY AT ICS

ICS' CORPORATE HEADQUARTERS IS LOCATED IN GLOUCESTER, ONTARIO.

Med-Eng Systems Inc.

As a world leader in the research, design, and production o personal protective equipment, Med-Eng Systems Inc. focuses on the devel opment of superior protective systems, with an emphasis on educating th end user about its products and how best to use them. For those reasons, the company occupies a commanding share of protective equipment markets, and has its products trusted in more than 130 countries and territories around the world.

THE STORY OF MED-ENG dates back to 1981 and the company's cofounder and president, Richard L'Abbé. At the time, his first challenge would be substantial; only three months to design and build a new explosive ordnance disposal (EOD) helmet for the Royal Canadian Mounted Police (RCMP). The helmet delivered a technological quantum leap, overshadowing anything else available in the world in terms of versatility and protection. Med-Eng was born.

Med-Eng's growth continued when its helmet was bundled with a bomb disposal suit from another Canadian supplier. But the friendly relations would not last, after a foreign competitor bought out the suit manufacturer and expected Med-Eng to quietly disappear. Instead, this served to spark a fire on the company's research and development (R & D) efforts, and soon Med-Eng embarked upon an aggressive program to pioneer research into blast effects on the human body. The result was a fully integrated suit and helmet ensemble, and the ability to present the market with a protective solution based on the latest empirical science.

The lean years of Med-Eng's intense R & D efforts and the hostile market environment were rewarded by a stunning success in the international military and law enforcement communities. This set up a rapid expansion into the United States, where the firm quickly overtook its larger American competitors. Giving confidence in his products a new meaning, L'Abbé subjected himself to explosions in 19 successful tests and earned the trust of previously skeptical clients. No competitor has ever accepted this challenge in its own suits, and Med-Eng had caught the world's attention. Today the company retains more than 90 percent of the world marke for EOD ensembles.

Not content with the firm's success in only one market, however, the Med-Eng team decided to apply its leading knowledge to other arenas. In the field of anti-personnel land mine protection, for example, several innovative protective systems - including the "Spider Boot," a world-famous, top-performing foot protection system - were developed to with-stand the smaller blast threats of mines. The company also addressed the blast threats of chemical and biological weapons associated with terrorist explosive devices, and developed remote handling tools designed for delicate bomb disposal operations.

THE KEY TO MED-ENG'S achievements over the years is the firm's holistic approach to R & D, as shown by its V•Top line of protective equipment for public and prison riots. Starting from a clear understanding of the user's needs and circumstances, the Design Engineering team sought to find that elusive optimal balance between comfort and protection against blunt impacts. This investigation also included a thorough understanding of crowd management psychology studies. The result is an integrated system that provides superior protection,

The key to Med-Eng's success over the years is the firm's holistic approach to research and development.

›ut is worn under flame resistant ›overalls to minimize any provocative ıppearances. In turn, this is ıccompanied by a technical ›resentation that helps police ınderstand how they can deploy in ı non-threatening manner, secure n the confidence they have in heir protective equipment and raining. In the end, peaceful ›rotests are far less likely to legenerate into violence, and ›olice are praised for their tolerance ınd restraint.

The latest rising star for Med-Eng s quickly proving to be a suite of ›ersonal cooling systems. These systems are aimed at people vorking in conditions of intense ıeat stress, ranging from heavy ndustry to law enforcement. The ›eauty of this technology lies in its inely tuned ability to mimic the ›ody's natural temperature regula-:ion system. Already the system ıas been used in several extreme :onditions, such as Formula 1 and NASCAR auto racing, and high-risk hazardous materials operations. What binds these applications is their demand for a reliable, safe and effective method of reducing the very serious risks of heat stress. By any measure, the commercial opportunities for this product line are almost limitless indeed.

SHARING KNOWLEDGE TO INCREASE USER SAFETY

In each of these markets, one critical factor that has always distinguished Med-Eng from its competitors has been an unfailing commitment to sharing its research findings with end users. This co-operative and forthright approach includes published test reports, high speed video and now 3D animations. These techniques have gained the respect of clients the world over as they apply their newfound insights towards improved operational techniques. In this manner, Med-Eng has not only contributed to internationally recognized standards for protective equipment, but has defined the term "Engineered by Med-Eng" as a mark of knowledge and superior performance.

The foundation of success for Med-Eng is now well proven: an ability to advance the science of personal protection, transform this knowledge into superior products across divergent markets, and develop global client partnerships. So it is not surprising the brilliant future of this rapidly growing company that has caught the eye of so many, given the ever-increasing array of threats to personal safety in the world's extreme environments.

New threats will need to be understood. New protective technologies will be demanded. And the developers of these solutions will be held to a higher standard than ever before. But these are the very challenges at which Med-Eng excels and will surely continue to do so for years to come.

Tessier Translations Corporation

MORE THAN JUST ANOTHER TRANSLATION FIRM, TESSIER TRANSLATION Corporation is an institution in Ottawa. When it comes to professiona translation services, Tessier sets the standards–and delivers. While there ar other translation providers in the Capital, Tessier has carved a special nich for itself as an industry leader. ✱ Translation is big business in Ottawa. Wit the *Official Languages Act*, NAFTA, the ever-growing importance of international trade, and Canada's commitment to multiculturalism, the need for translation has never been greater.

When translating copy, Tessier Translations' job is not to attempt to refine, embellish, or enhance the material supplied by the client, but to accurately reflect in the other language the exact sense and tone of the original, as the author meant it to be. "One should not expect us to rewrite or edit the copy submitted for translation," says company President Philippe Tessier. "Our clients expect us to render their original text exactly as they wrote it in the first place–no more, no less. They are the ones who know their business, and what they are talking about. We are not there to pass judgment on their knowledge of the subject matter, their writing skills, or their ability to communicate effectively. Our role is delivering–and not creating–a message."

A quote from the *Concise Oxford French Dictionary* sums up Tessier's philosophy: "The value of a good translation lies in the similarity of its impact on the French mind with the impact of the original on the English mind." In essence, this is exactly what Tessier Translations has been all about since 1981 in the National Capital: providing accurate translations that convey identical messages to the reader in both languages.

CLOCKWISE FROM TOP: (FROM LEFT) JOHANNE ST-ONGE, SECRETARY-TREASURER; PHILIPPE TESSIER, PRESIDENT; AND ALAIN BÉLANGER, VICE-PRESIDENT, REVIEW TESSIER TRANSLATIONS' PRODUCTION SCHEDULE DURING AN AFTERNOON HUDDLE AT THE COMPANY'S DOWNTOWN OTTAWA OFFICES. TESSIER HANDLES MORE THAN 70,000 PAGES OF TRANSLATION COPY ANNUALLY.

TESSIER'S TRANSLATORS HAVE THEIR OWN LIBRARY AND DOCUMENTATION CENTRE ON-SITE. WITH DIRECT ACCESS TO ALL NECESSARY DOCUMENTS, PROFESSIONAL LIBRARIAN JO-ANNE LORTIE AND HER COLLEAGUES ARE ABLE TO PROVIDE INFORMATION INSTANTLY TO ALL TRANSLATORS, AT THEIR REQUEST.

WORKING ON THE PREMISES AT TESSIER TRANSLATIONS, PROFESSIONAL TRANSLATOR LISE LEVESQUE USES DICTATION EQUIPMENT TO TRANSLATE DIRECTLY FROM THE ORIGINAL MANUSCRIPT SUPPLIED BY THE CLIENT.

70,000 PAGES ANNUALLY AND COUNTING

Philippe Tessier himself is no stranger to translation. Prior to starting Tessier Translations, he spent 19 years in the translation sector of th federal government. Over the years his business grew from a single-man basement operation to a full-size company with key associates Alain Bélanger as vice-president and Johanne St-Onge as secretary-treasurer. Senior Translators Miche Cardin and Claudette Vaillancourt also sit on the company's Board of Directors. Tessier considers all four to be responsible for the company's success.

◀ INNOVACOM MARKETING & COMMUNICATION

he public sector accounts for a zable percentage of the company's usiness, but is by no means the rgest, despite the close proximity f key federal government departents. Over the years, Tessier ranslations has developed a tightly nit network of contacts, and a gnificant body of knowledge in everal areas of public and business dministration, legislation, science nd technology, agriculture, education, environment, health and medine, customs, taxation, immigration, stice, law, dairy products, international trade, marketing, banking, surance, accounting, industrial nd labour relations, human resources, nd nuclear energy.

n total, the company handles a aggering 20 million words, which acks up to more than 70,000 ages of text annually. And Tessier ys that the local market has yet be tapped to its full potential.

QUALITY, TIMELINESS, AND CONSISTENCY

Quick turnaround and efficiency keeps clients coming back. Every professional on the 45-plus staff understands the business of translation, and each has his or her own areas of specialty. The team of full-time salaried employees–translators, word processing operators, research staff, administrative support staff, and systems people–uses state-of-the-art research tools and cutting-edge technology to ensure fast turnaround time.

Quality is a top priority as well. As important as conveying the same message to all audiences is delivering the finished product to the client's exact specifications. Tessier Translations regularly updates its terminology and style databases on each of its clients. When a job comes in, translators can quickly look up the style and special terminology that are essential to each client. The client may even request special job-specific instructions that deviate from its normal standards.

Tessier Translations is in business to serve clients. To this end, Philippe Tessier is dedicated to one rule: "We always meet and exceed client expectations." This speaks volumes to the commitment the company makes to its clients: that it is highly reliable, consistent, and organized, and that it will always produce quality work–on time and on budget.

It may come as little surprise that Tessier Translations has been honoured for its outstanding record of professional achievements and contributions to quality linguistic services, and for its involvement in the community as a contributor to student scholarships with both the University of Ottawa Translation School and the Université du Québec à Hull.

When asked what accomplishment he is most proud of, Philippe Tessier points to the fact that Tessier Translations has become synonymous with high-quality professional translation in the National Capital and beyond. Tessier Translations Corporation has worked hard to position itself at the leading edge of professional translation in Ottawa–no small feat indeed. And through its hard work, top-notch resources, exceptionally dedicated staff, and a total commitment to customer service, it is no surprise that the firm consistently dominates the translation industry in Ottawa.

A busy pool of 12 Tessier word processing operators types up the draft copy as it is fed from the dictating machines used by the translators. Dictation saves translators time and speeds up production.

Tessier word processing services supervisor Annie Fortin ensures that deadlines are met and that a quality product is delivered to clients. The firm handles both government work and corporate translation needs.

Novotel Ottawa

NOVOTEL OTTAWA IS ONE OF THE CITY'S MORE FAMOUS DESTINATION for tourists and business travellers alike. Located in the heart of Ottawa vibrant downtown area, the hotel is conveniently located near some c the city's most recognizable landmarks, including the Rideau Cana Parliament Hill, the first Carleton County Jail and Courthouse, th Byward Market, and the Ottawa Congress Centre.

A five-minute walk from the downtown business district and shopping on historical Sparks Street, the hotel is also close to many of the city's finest restaurants, as well as to museums and the National Gallery of Canada.

A STORIED PAST

The story of the Novotel Ottawa is one that spans more than 150 years. The current hotel is managed by Accor Hotels, who transformed the old Albion Hotel into the Novotel in 1988.

For its part, the Albion Hotel predates Canadian Confederation. Founded in 1844 by local businessman Allan Cameron, the hotel was originally located across from the first Carleton County Jail and Courthouse. Its clientele included a good number of courthouse dignitaries and students.

The only part of the original hote that remains today is an addition constructed in 1871. That section of the building, which houses Cafe Nicole, Novotel's restaurant, was designated a heritage site by the City of Ottawa in 1984. The plaque out side the heritage addition states that the former Albion Hotel was a meeting place in old Bytown for sports enthusiasts who came to watch prizefights staged in the dir ing room as well as many other groups.

▼ JEAN GUICHARD

LOCATED IN THE HEART OF OTTAWA'S VIBRANT DOWNTOWN AREA, THE NOVOTEL OTTAWA IS ONE OF THE CITY'S MORE FAMOUS DESTINATIONS AND IS CONVENIENTLY LOCATED NEAR SOME OF THE CITY'S MOST RECOGNIZABLE LANDMARKS.

Since that time, much of the landscape around the old Albion Hote has changed dramatically. The old county jail, where Canada's last stat execution took place, now serves as a youth hostel. Across Rideau Street, the Rideau Centre is one o the city's premier shopping destinations for residents and visitors t Ottawa alike, and the Rideau Cana is one of the world's longest outdoor skating rinks.

NOVOTEL OTTAWA TODAY

Of course, the physical structure of the old Albion Hotel itself has changed, too. The main portion o the new Novotel Ottawa is a nine-storey, 281-room modern facility. The hotel offers to the individual tourist and business traveller amen ties that include 24-hour exercise facilities, a swimming pool, a sauna a steam room, a java bar, and a whirlpool tub. The hotel's eight meeting rooms range in capacity from 10 to 160 people, and are fully catered by the hotel restaurant. A link joins the main body o the hotel to the heritage building and Café Nicole.

Novotel Ottawa's guests' comfort, quite clearly, is very important to the hotel's owners. In that sense, a Accor hotels are subject to regular renovations and preventive mainte nance in order to maintain exacting quality standards.

▲ JEAN GUICHARD

Novotel Ottawa's guests' comfort, quite clearly, is very important to the hotel's owners. All Accor hotels are subject to regular renovations and preventive maintenance to maintain exacting quality standards.

ovotel Ottawa underwent a major enovation in 1996, when all rooms ere upgraded with new beds; new arpeting and wallpaper; and a fresh, ew décor with new colours. The sult is a comfortable, tranquil destiation for Ottawa's visitors. Renoations to the hotel continue today, elping to make it a home-awayom-home destination for travellers.

AFÉ NICOLE

he centrepiece of Novotel Ottawa Café Nicole. Located in the origial Albion Hotel building, it is a ll restaurant decorated in attractive astel blues and oranges. The walls nd menus are decorated with ainted murals and other artwork roduced by local artists, and the enu offers a selection of French editerranean cuisine.

hefs at Café Nicole are specially ained to prepare meals to the ghest standards, which guests have come to expect from Novotel hotels around the world. The menu is updated and changed every six to eight months, and is set by Accor Hotels' head office.

THE HIGHEST STANDARDS IN CUSTOMER SERVICE

There is very much a family orientation to Novotel Ottawa. Staff members work as a close-knit unit and rely on one another for help. They truly create a friendly atmosphere for the guests. Attention to customers' needs is what makes for a better product at the Novotel Ottawa, which means that staff at the hotel are committed to being the best, and work continuously to improve their service in any way possible.

Novotel's attention to customer service has not been lost on visitors to Ottawa, either. The hotel has become a destination spot for some of Ottawa's more famous visitors. Many entertainers–among them Glass Tiger, David Suzuki, Alannah Myles, Roger Whittaker, Colin James, and R & B group TLC–have called the hotel home during their respective stays in Ottawa.

The hotel's entire staff of some 100 workers is fluently bilingual, making the hotel an attractive option to foreign travellers. Staff members make sure that all guests' needs are looked after, and will help arrange an evening or a day out for guests–to the National Arts Centre, the Corel Centre for some exciting National Hockey League action, or some other venue of interest.

The end result of the shared commitment to customer service by the staff at Novotel Ottawa is a comfortable environment in which guests feel as though the hotel is a home away from home.

INFORMATION TECHNOLOGY (IT) HAS REVOLUTIONIZED THE BUSINESS world since the 1970s, but there continue to be many challenges in manag ing the rapid evolution of technology. In the 1998 book entitled *The Smar Way to Buy Information Technology*, authors Brad L. Peterson and Diane M Carco point to many of the IT-related problems facing organizations today These problems include technological complexity and rapid change, competing standards, incompatible vendor solutions, islands of automation, and fragmented IT resources.

THE TECHNO-JUNGLE

Organizations are faced with integrating an entire alphabet soup of technologies such as XML, SOAP, z/OS, Unix, TCP/IP, ITIL, W2K, JAVA, SNA, SAN, LAN, WAN, MAN, Metaframe, NT, HTTP, XP, WebSphere, EJB, VB, PDF, JPEG, and Gigabit Ethernet to name just a few. Bill Carico, a well-known industry observer and president of the U.S.-based consulting company ACTS Corporation, refers to this environment aptly as the techno-jungle.

The Powell Group, and the entire IT professional services industry, fills a market need for specialized expertise to help organizations deal with the complex undergrowth of interrelated technologies found in most modern organizations. Some of the services provided by the Powell Group include management and technical consulting, functional outsourcing, help desk management, and application development.

Founded in 1991 by Donald R. Powell, the Powell Group has become one of the most well established IT professional services companies in the national capital region, with annual revenues nearing $30 millior and a staff of some 200 employees and associates. Services are providec to all of the larger Government of Canada departments and agencies, many Crown corporations, and a large number of private sector companies in the Ottawa area and the United States.

The Powell Group has become one of the most well established information technology companies in the Ottawa area (top).

The Powell Group spring reception is eagerly anticipated each year by the Ottawa information technology community as a great place to network and meet old friends (bottom).

RICHARD FOULDS

AN EFFECTIVE BUSINESS MODEL

The Powell Group has evolved a unique and successful business model that consists of four distinct companies: TPG Technology Consulting, Logic 2000 Inc., Wilcom Systems Ltd., and Marketware Corporation.

TPG Technology Consulting provides a full range of IT services, witl emphasis on enterprise systems anc data centre environments. Logic 2000 Inc. is a professional services firm that assists clients with custom application development and network consulting services. Wilcom Systems Ltd. also provides a range of IT services, including technical support, with an emphasis on business continuity and help desk solutions. Marketware Corporation provides services to the automotiv aftermarket in the United States and Canada.

The Powell Group has also developed a highly effective general approach to the IT industry. Senior management is located in Ottawa, allowing key decisions to be made locally. In addition, the company has always kept overheads low, providing excellent value to clients. The company has also maintained its independence from product vendors, ensuring that technology recommendations are impartial. Another consideration is that the company makes use of both employees and subcontractors, providing the widest choice of scarce best-of-breed technical resources. One of the company's greatest strengths is the demonstrated ability to work co-operatively with both client resources and other vendors to achieve optimum results for clients. The Powell Group is also a founding member of CABiNET, an Ottawa-based association of IT professional services companies.

In every consulting assignment, the Powell Group attempts to balance the contribution and obligations of the client, the individual doing the work, and the company.

LONG-TERM CUSTOMER RELATIONSHIPS

The Powell Group's approach to business has proved to be very effective in meeting client requirements, and the company has developed long-term relationships with a number of major clients. Some of the most significant relationships include the 1999 awarding of a large, multiyear contract for engineering and technical support for the Government Telecommunications and Informatics Service (GTIS), a government organization that provides shared IT services to the federal government; being selected as one of only five professional services vendors to meet the requirements of the Canada Customs and Revenue Agency (CCRA) for a three-year period; and Marketware's signing of a three-year agreement to provide a parts catalogue and electronic data interchange (EDI) services to Tenneco Automotive, the large, U.S.-based manufacturer of Monroe shock absorbers and many other automotive products.

▸ COUVRETTE/OTTAWA

▸ COUVRETTE/OTTAWA

Dave Cole, Vice-President of Marketware, demonstrates the electronic commerce capabilities implemented for a major client (top).

Approaches proposed by the Powell Group provide practical, cost-effective solutions to real business problems and avoid technology as an end in itself (middle).

Don Powell meets with a key client, Fred McCallum, Director General of Network and Computer Services, the operational arm of the Government Telecommunications and Informatics Service organization (bottom).

The Powell Group was also selected as a service provider for the major Government of Canada initiative referred to as Government Online (GOL). GOL is a commitment by the federal government to provide all government services on the Internet for the benefit of all Canadians. GOL is just one example of the many business and technology challenges faced by organizations today as on-line access to services becomes increasingly prevalent.

Based on the Powell Group's proven track record and well-established position in the marketplace, the company's management and staff look forward to continuing success in meeting new client requirements well into the new century.

▸ COUVRETTE/OTTAWA

Expo Zone International Inc.

Expo Zone International Inc. is an award-winning fabrication company. Expo Zone specializes in the creation of museum and visitor centre exhibits, corporate interiors, trade show booths, portable displays, custom furnishings, and graphics. The company's impressive portfolio includes projects in Alaska, New York, Portugal, and Canada, with invitations to bid on projects in both Europe and Asia. Information on the company and its portfolio is available on its Web site, www.expo-zone.com.

In 1994, Expo Zone was established in Ottawa to be close to Canada's national museums and high-tech industry. The company's facilities house all fabrication trades under one roof, and the markets have responded enthusiastically to this approach to client service.

Expo Zone's experienced management and staff–working as a team–take pride in their work. All projects, big or small, are given the same consideration and attention. First and foremost, the Expo Zone team strives for quality in workmanship and service integrity. As a result, the company consistently delivers award-winning results that exceed client objectives.

Expo Zone International Inc. created exhibits for the Robert Moses Niagara Power Project Visitor Center in Niagara Falls, New York (top) and the Millennium Lobby of Place du Portage's Phase III in Hull, Quebec (bottom left); the company also created the JetForm Corporation custom trade show booth (bottom right).

The Fruits of Hard Labour

This hard work is paying off. In 1995, Expo Zone was selected as one of *Ottawa Business Magazine*'s five Rising Star companies. A year later, the Ottawa Carleton Board of Trade presented the company with its Silver Award for Business Achievement in the new business category. In 1997, the Gloucester Chamber of Commerce honoured the company with its Business of the Year Award. Expo Zone has also gained international recognition by winning four first place international awards at the Exhibitors Show in Las Vegas.

In the fall of 2000, to meet Expo Zone's expansion requirements and the needs of the Canadian Museum of Civilization, the two organizations entered into a contractual partner-

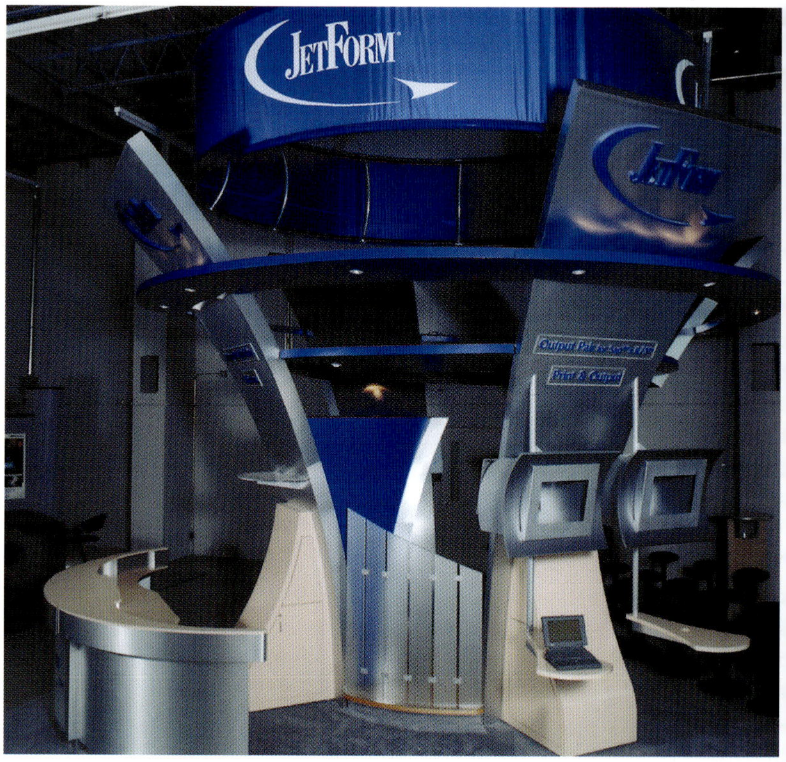

ship. Expo Zone is now responsible for this major museum's in-house fabrication shop. The partnership confirms Expo Zone's professional credibility and dedication to high-quality production.

THE OLD TRADES AND THE NEW ECONOMY

Fabrication specialists need to be masters of some of the world's oldest trades. Master craftsmen who produce the models, furniture, and landscape displays are in fact carpenters, cabinetmakers, metalworkers, painters, graphic artists, and sculptors. They combine old-world trades with modern communication technology to create effective displays.

Expo Zone has positioned itself as a world-class fabricator for the private and public sectors, and as an industry leader in innovation and service excellence. With exhibits in all of the major museums in the national capital region—as well as in visitor centres across North America—Expo Zone is fast becoming Canada's top expert custom fabricator.

For complete turnkey services, Expo Zone associates with other experts who share the same corporate philosophy toward client service. Examples of turnkey projects include the Canada Pavilion at Expo '98 in Lisbon, Canadian War Museum's Peacekeepers' Gallery, Kalamazoo Valley Science Center in Kalamazoo, and the Shania Twain Interpretive Centre in Timmins.

PARTNERS IN THE LOCAL ECONOMY

Since its inception, Expo Zone has successfully targeted Ottawa's twin engines for economic growth: the high-tech industry and the federal government. Both sectors participate in permanent museum, visitor centre, and lobby displays, as well as trade shows and conventions. All must be high-quality, eye-catching displays that will stop traffic and be informative. Trade shows must be portable, functional, and easy to set up and take down as well.

Marketing products and services at trade shows is essential for expansion into new markets. Successful organizations attend trade shows as part of their growth strategy to keep in touch with what is happening in their industry and show off their own achievements. Competitive marketing and promotion managers need top-quality entries on the trade show floor. Expo Zone provides them with the planning guidance to prevent oversights, while delivering first-class displays.

Expo Zone added the Canada and the World Visitor Centre in Ottawa to its portfolio.

SHOWING OFF ON THE WORLD STAGE

Canada has long had an international reputation for creating high-quality, successful exhibits. Expo 1967 in Montreal and Expo 1986 in Vancouver focussed all eyes on Canada and the talent within its borders. Canadian firms have continued to be sought-after in the world exhibit market.

From 1997 to 2001, Expo Zone experienced a 40 percent annual growth rate as the company's work continued to achieve recognition. The firm's quality, integrity, and dedication to service continue to ensure repeat business and attract new clients.

Expo Zone has produced and installed exhibits in all regions of Canada, including the remote regions of Nunavut and Newfoundland. Recently turning its focus on the U.S. markets, Expo Zone has completed multimillion-dollar projects in Alaska, New York, and Michigan. The company's trade show division has now expanded to include service to U.S., South American, and European markets.

In 2001, Expo Zone International Inc. was developing business with other firms in Canada and the United States. This exchange was profitable, and the future looks bright for negotiating other business associations and joint venture opportunities. Expo Zone continues to be a rising star in its field.

Expo Zone is recognized for the quality of its workmanship.

Catena Networks

CONSIDER FOR A MOMENT THE GROWTH OF THE INTERNET SINCE 1990. In the early 1990s, it was a relatively unexplored commodity. Many people had access to the technology, but it was still in its formative stages. Contrast that with the prevalence of the technology today. While the growth of voice traffic on conventional phone lines has tapered off, data traffic is growing at a staggering rate and has already exceeded the volume of voice traffic.

Catena Networks' Chairman of the Board Jim Hjartarson is also one of the firm's founders.

It was in December 1998 that the five founding team members of Catena Networks began to recognize the Internet's potential to transform the way people live, work, and play. The drive behind their move to create the start-up company was simple: they wanted to make high-speed Internet access as available, affordable, and reliable as plain old telephone service (POTS) is today.

EVERYONE WANTS BROADBAND

Since 1998, Catena's mandate has been to develop the solutions that will enable the consumer mass-market deployment of broadband digital subscriber line (DSL) services. The challenge is that today's DSL data access network is being designed as a separate overlay to the voice network. This data overlay network is satisfactory for the deployment of niche, business-oriented services, but it is not scalable for price-sensitive consumer mass-market deployment.

Enter Catena's two newest products, the CNX-5 Broadband Asymmetric Digital Subscriber Line (ADSL) System and the CN1000 Broadband Loop Carrier (BLC)–both of which will enable carriers to accelerate the volume deployment of broadband DSL services.

"We have integrated ADSL and POTS technologies at the silicon level," says Jim Hjartarson, Chairman of the Board of Catena Networks and one of the firm's founders. "Consequently, we can develop system solutions that enable service providers to deliver fully integrated voice and data services to subscribers more quickly, cost effectively, and profitably than ever before."

Catena Networks' research and development facility is located on Legget Drive in Kanata.

Catena has been selling its CNX-5 system to facilities-based carriers, which are using it to upgrade their large installed base of Lucent SLC-5 Digital Loop Carrier Systems in remote terminals. The CNX-5 enables carriers to deliver POTS and ADSL services on any copper pair, without reducing the number of available POTS lines. Installation involves little more than a simple card-for-card replacement that provides two lines of integrated POTS and ADSL.

Catena's two newest products—the CNX-5 Broadband ADSL System (left) and the CN1000 Broadband Loop Carrier (right)—will enable carriers to accelerate the volume deployment of broadband DSL services.

Catena also is marketing its CN1000 BLC, a new class of access system that will enable carriers to accelerate DSL service delivery and smoothly migrate from today's circuit-based public switched telephone network (PSTN) to a converged, packet-based public network. By integrating POTS and DSL on every line, at POTS economics, the CN1000 helps service providers dramatically reduce their capital and operations costs. The CN1000 also enables no-truck-roll, remote DSL provisioning.

NOT AN AVERAGE YOUNG COMPANY

Though its customer base primarily consists of facilities-based carriers in North America, Catena has plans to expand its operations overseas—such is the demand for broadband services today and in the immediate future. Hjartarson says that the company "is not your average young company," in the sense that it has a large internal team dedicated to developing solutions that will enable the mass-market deployment of broadband DSL services.

"It's a credit to everyone who works here that this company has reached the point it is at today," Hjartarson says. "In the beginning, many people said that it was impossible to develop this type of technology, so it was a big leap of faith for everyone who came to work here. But there is no question that Catena would not be where it is today without the hard work of everyone involved."

All members of Catena Networks' founding team are alumni from Ottawa's technology industry. It was for that reason that the firm decided to lay roots in the city, though its corporate headquarters is located in Redwood Shores, California. The pool of talent from which Catena has drawn its employees, combined with a strong core of investors who see Ottawa as one of the world leaders in high-technology development, has made Catena's campus on Legget Drive in Kanata the heartbeat of the firm's operations.

"As one of this company's founding members, I'm most proud of the fact that we have been able to meet our investors' expectations at every stage of development," says Hjartarson. "We have always delivered on our promises, and we have done so on budget. Meeting those criteria has put us on a path to success."

The Ottawa Partnership (TOP) is a group of leaders from the public and private sectors who provide strategic advice to the City of Ottawa on growing and sustaining the local economy. Founded in 1999 and co-chaired by Mayor Bob Chiarelli and Kirk Mandy, Vice Chairman of Zarlink Semiconductor Inc.

TOP plays a key role in shaping the policies to guide Ottawa's economic future.

In 2000, it released a landmark study called *Choosing a Future: A New Economic Vision for the City of Ottawa*–also known as the Economic Generators Initiative–to provide a roadmap for developing the key economic clusters, or generators, that fuel the city's growth. Since then, TOP has built on the success of this study, most recently coordinating a second major report which has helped guide development of a long-term economic strategy for the City of Ottawa.

TOP's co-chairs Kirk Mandy (left) and Mayor Bob Chiarelli.

PUBLIC SECTOR RESOURCES, PRIVATE SECTOR KNOWLEDGE

TOP was born of an agreement among business leaders and economic agencies to align their efforts to promote the overall well-being of the city's economy. Its philosophy is simple: Ottawa intends to remain among the top-performing regions in the world and must think strategically to meet the challenges of global competition.

TOP is made up of community leaders from City Council (the Mayor and one councillor), the private sector (heads of local businesses), representatives from industry associations, local chambers of commerce and post-secondary institutions, and several ex-officio members.

"The business community recognizes that acting together and speaking with one voice can have a very positive effect on making the right strategic decisions and building public support for the direction chosen," says Kirk Mandy. "TOP is an important forum for business and community leaders to develop a clear and consistent position on key issues."

TOP serves as an advisory body to city government by providing input and making recommendations on important matters, such as infrastructure development, or education and training programs, that could affect the business climate.

"Ottawa's business community is highly civic-minded," says Mayor Chiarelli. "The willingness of senior business leaders to sit on the TOP board and provide advice, at a very strategic level, on what needs to be done to grow and sustain the local economy has been fundamental to our city's success. This culture of collaboration is one of our most important advantages."

Ottawa is one of several world-leading cities, including Austin, Texas, and Singapore, that have adopted a collaborative model for economic development. These cities have discovered that leaders can positively influence their economic future by working together.

"Business leaders recognize that Ottawa is a dynamic city with a high quality of life, and that this is a key part of their success," says

Ottawa's business leaders work to generate a high-performance economy based on investment, entrepreneurship, and innovation.

Mandy. "TOP is a forum that allows businesses to play a role in building on these strengths."

Generating Growth

The 2000 Economic Generators initiative identified seven export-based clusters as crucial to the city's continued growth and prosperity: software and communication services; microelectronics; life sciences; professional services; photonics; tourism; and telecommunications equipment.

The report also demonstrated the link between the success of these export clusters and the strength of the city's local economy. Cluster companies create jobs and contribute to Ottawa's high quality of life by hiring employees who buy homes, cars and appliances and eat in local restaurants. The City of Ottawa has officially adopted the cluster-based approach as its main economic development strategy.

Since then, the Economic Generators Initiative has fueled a wide range of economic successes, including projects to raise Ottawa's international profile, create cluster-based business incubators, build Ottawa's talent pool, and develop a vision and strategy for city-wide, high-speed broadband access.

TOP has taken these successes a step further by coordinating development of *Innovation Ottawa: A Strategy for Sustaining Economic Generators*. Unveiled November 13, 2002, this report provided the City of Ottawa with a series of recommendations for advancing the export-based economic clusters and enhancing the region's innovation pipeline. It calls on local business and industry leaders to harness their competitiveness and create a strong innovation pipeline to accelerate discovery, development, and deployment of products and services for export.

Continued Competitive Excellence

Most recently, TOP has taken a leadership role in the creation of a long-term economic strategy as part of the City's Ottawa 20/20 growth management initiative–a vision for planning where Ottawa is headed over the next 20 years and how it will get there.

Approved April 23, 2003, by City Council, the *Ottawa 20/20 Economic Strategy* provides a clear vision and set of 26 policy directions that will ensure Ottawa's continued competitiveness and prosperity. The strategy reinforces the importance of the city's economic clusters and the economic foundations that support them, while at the same time, identifies strategies to support Ottawa's broader economy.

Along with the Economic Strategy are two key supporting plans: a *Broadband Plan*, which provides a road map for ensuring that Ottawa's vision of universal broadband services throughout the city becomes a reality within the next five years; and a *Talent Plan*, which details the city's strategy to link employers to a skilled workforce and to improve workforce infrastructure.

Tangible results are being seen already. Various initiatives are underway including projects to increase the commercialization of local research and technology, extend broadband service to every resident, and strengthen industry cluster collaboration.

With the roadmap firmly in place, TOP will focus its attention over the coming months on monitoring the implementation of the economic strategy and its supporting plans, and on identifying further actions to maintain and enhance Ottawa's competitiveness, prosperity and quality of life.

"Our economic vision for the year 2020 is an Ottawa that is prosperous, innovative, entrepreneurial, and recognized around the world for its economic and technology leadership," says Chiarelli. "Ottawa is one of the world's best-kept secrets. But the story of our success is spreading quickly."

Hydro Ottawa Holding Inc.

Hydro Ottawa Holding Inc. was incorporated on November 1, 2000, as a brand new business. The company and its predecessors have been an integral part of the growth and success of this world-class city for almost a century.

Municipal restructuring and changes in the electricity marketplace in Ontario necessitated the merging of five local utilities and the establishment of a new corporate structure.

Hydro Ottawa Holding Inc., through its board of directors and senior management, provides strategic direction to three affiliates: Hydro Ottawa Limited, Energy Ottawa Inc. and Telecom Ottawa Limited. Through its affiliates, Hydro Ottawa is committed to finding new and innovative ways to leverage its capabilities, improve productivity, and focus on customer service excellence that will achieve sustainable business growth and increased shareholder value.

HYDRO OTTAWA LIMITED

Hydro Ottawa Limited is Ottawa's electricity distribution company. As Ontario's second-largest municipal distribution company, Hydro Ottawa Limited has two core responsibilities. First, they ensure a safe, reliable delivery of electricity to 265,000 customers in the city of Ottawa and the village of Casselman. Second, Hydro Ottawa Limited bills for its services and for the services provided by other organizations in Ontario's electricity system.

Cost and reliability are the two measures by which customers judge their distributor's performance. To that end, Hydro Ottawa's rates are the lowest in the province. In terms of reliability, Hydro Ottawa consistently ranks among the best in the country as measured by the Canadian Electricity Association.

◀ WILLIAM P. MCELLIGOTT PHOTOGRAPHY

The company's line crews and equipment are second to none. Their skills were proven through one of the worst natural disasters of the 20th century–the Great Ice Storm of 1998–which paralyzed most of northeastern North America and left many people without power for weeks in freezing cold temperatures. Hydro Ottawa crews worked day and night in horrendous conditions, and were able to limit power outages in most cases to hours; a testament to an organization that understands what really matters to customers.

The year 2002 saw the official launch of two affiliates: Energy Ottawa Inc. and Telecom Ottawa Limited. Both have had outstanding success and attracted international attention.

Clockwise from top:
Hydro Ottawa is powered by people. The company's performance measurement and incentive programs are designed to promote excellence and position the corporation as an employer of choice.

Hydro Ottawa's team takes great pride in being plugged into the community. Bucket truck rides are a favourite with kids and staff alike.

Telecom Ottawa Limited is poised for expansion providing bandwidth in much the same way other utilities provide water or power – available all the time, as much as needed, reliably, and at prices that make sense.

NERGY OTTAWA INC.

GESTION CONSEIL S.C.P. INC.

Energy Ottawa's Chaudière Falls Generating Station, a historic landmark, uses state-of-the-art technology to maximize output and earn the official designation "Green Power" through Environment Canada's Environmental Choice Program (left).

Hydro Ottawa's reputation for reliability and safety is at the core of everything the company does and is the key to its success. (right)

Energy Ottawa Inc. is a diversified and innovative energy company that generates "green" power, provides hot water services to approximately 40,000 customers, and offers a growing range of energy management and procurement services.

Energy Ottawa operates two generating stations located on the Ottawa River, adjacent to Chaudière Falls. In 2001, both generating stations became privileged members of Environment Canada's Environmental Choice Program (ECP), which recognizes higher standards of environmental performance by certifying "green" products and services. These century-old power plants have been refurbished and automated, increasing their capacity by 60% to 15 megawatts and displacing the equivalent of 88,000 tonnes of greenhouse gas emissions per year. As a producer of "green" power, Energy Ottawa has been awarded Environment Canada's EcoLogo certification and was short-listed for the prestigious Global Energy Award. Chaudière is one of a select few environmental leaders in Ontario that offer water-powered, alternative-source electricity.

TELECOM OTTAWA LIMITED

Telecom Ottawa is a broadband data utility that provides networking bandwidth and Internet services to businesses and public organizations throughout the Ottawa region. Telecom Ottawa owns and operates the all-optical communications backbone that protects and controls the electricity system in the Ottawa region. This constantly expanding system consists of some 300 kilometres of fiber-optic network that connects major institutions, businesses, government departments and public-sector agencies.

Because of its 'glass plumbing' assets–its fiber-optic backbone, enhanced by state-of-the art Ethernet networking technology–Telecom Ottawa is positioned today to be a leader in Ottawa in the provision of broadband data services on a "utility basis." This means Telecom Ottawa provides bandwidth in much the same way as other utilities provide water or power–available all the time, as much as needed, reliably, at prices that make sense.

Delivering broadband data capacity is a growth market in Ottawa which, compared to other Ontario metro regions, is somewhat underserved for affordable high-speed bandwidth. Telecom Ottawa's visions includes expanding its network footprint out into suburbs and communities beyond the downtown core. Where feasible, the company intends to be a strategic provider of bandwidth to community/public organizations located in areas of the Ottawa region where other providers have not yet deployed fiber.

PLUGGED INTO THE COMMUNITY

Hydro Ottawa Holding Inc.'s corporate culture instills a strong commitment not only to customer service, but also to community service. A dynamic team of 500 employees is the driving force behind their success. The company understands and acknowledges the importance of supporting its people as they contribute countless hours to improving the quality of life of those around them. As a corporate citizen, Hydro Ottawa Holding Inc. is proud of the partnerships it is continually developing with the community.

A BRIGHT FUTURE

As the city of Ottawa continues to grow and prosper, Hydro Ottawa Holding Inc. and its affiliates will pursue new opportunities, whenever they fit with its core businesses. The coming years will introduce many challenges and significant business decisions through which Hydro Ottawa Holding Inc. will continue to focus on customer excellence, productivity and growth.

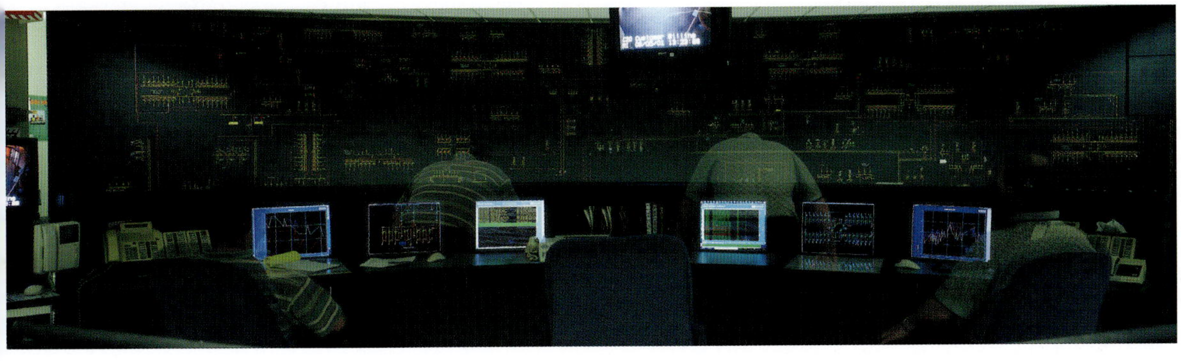

State-of-the-art facilities like Hydro Ottawa's System Control Centre allow the company to manage the power needs of the nation's capital 24 hours a day, seven days a week, 365 days of the year.

Index of Profiles